SCOTLAND BEFORE HISTORY

SCOTLAND
BEFORE HISTORY

STUART PIGGOTT
CBE D.LITT FBA

*with a Gazetteer of Ancient Monuments
by Graham Ritchie*

Polygon
EDINBURGH

© Stuart Piggott 1982

First published by
Edinburgh University Press
22 George Square, Edinburgh

Reprinted 1992 by Polygon

Set by Speedspools, Edinburgh
and printed in Great Britain by
Redwood Press Limited, Melksham, Wiltshire

British Library Cataloguing
    in Publication Data
Piggott, Stuart
Scotland before history
1. Scotland – History – to 1057
I. Title
941.101   DA770

ISBN 0 7486 6067 4

Frontispiece:
Recumbent stone circle, Easter Aquorthies, Aberdeen

CONTENTS

PREFACE

The text of this book, which is no more than a long essay divided into five parts, is an attempt to present in non-technical language the story of human settlement and development in what is now Scotland from the earliest times to the Roman Occupation. This story, recovered almost entirely by the techniques of archaeology, is not only imperfect and full of gaps, but provisional pending further research. The main lines appear reasonably certain, however, and give some indication of the prehistoric contribution to what was to become the earliest historic Scotland.

First published some twenty-five years ago, this essay has been revised at the suggestion of Edinburgh University Press, but it remains in large measure as originally conceived.

I invited Graham Ritchie to collaborate with me on the revision of the text, and gladly acknowledge his valuable assistance. The select gazetteer of some of the best-preserved prehistoric sites in Scotland has been provided by him, at the invitation of the Press, as have the illustrations. In the course of revision we have benefited from the help of Anne Turnbull, and in the preparation of the gazetteer, from the advice of Anna Ritchie and Stratford Halliday.

Stuart Piggott

I

To understand a people, one must first understand their country. Without a knowledge of the routes of access and of egress by land and sea, of the regions of mountain and moorland over against those of forest and flood plain, of the conditions of climate and natural environment – in a word, without a geographical setting – any study of human communities in past or present times must be a meaningless abstraction. Our concern here is with people who, by migration and settlement, adaptation and contrivance, created the population and texture of society, upon which the historical kingdoms of ancient and more recent Scotland were based. If we are to attempt to understand the nameless peoples of antiquity, ancestors of those who, in the beginnings of history, were to be known as Scots or Picts, Angles or Britons, we must consider them in relation to the lands in which they lived, and to the landscape they helped to shape. For apart from the bleak mountain masses and some moorlands and sand dunes, the scenery of Scotland, like that of most of Europe, is man-made, the culmination of processes of husbandry and exploitation

which began more than nine thousand years ago.

Let us begin by reminding ourselves that the British Isles form a north-westerly outpost of the European continent, from which they were finally severed by the formation of the English Channel in approximately its present form about 8,500 years ago. As far as the human habitation of Scotland is concerned, there is hardly any evidence of even the presence of man in the more northerly parts of Britain before at the earliest the seventh millennium B C, at a time when the Scottish coastline, with interesting minor exceptions, had already settled down to its present form. For our purposes then the basic geographical structure of modern Scotland was that which influenced (and sometimes decisively determined) the pattern of settlement and the lines of communication in prehistoric antiquity.

These dates, and most which follow, are obtained by the now familiar radiocarbon or C-14 method. Radiocarbon dating depends on scientific principles which are in themselves simple, even if their application may be full of complexities. The earth's atmosphere, bombarded by ever-present cosmic radiation, contains as a result a small proportion of radioactive atoms, some of which are the variants, or isotopes, of common elements such as the carbon contained in the gas carbon dioxide. The radioactive isotope has an atomic weight of 14, as against 12 for normal carbon, and so has become known as 'C-14'. Being radioactive, it 'decays' by a steady loss of electrons to become nitrogen, so that the point at which half the radioactive content remains (the 'half-life') can be calculated, and is in this case about 5,500 years. All living matter on the planet absorbs C-14 and holds it in a small and fixed proportion, but on the death of the plant or animal the intake stops, and the radioactive carbon begins its decay at the known rate. Laboratory techniques can measure this in an appropriate sample of wood, charcoal, bone and so on, as the number of years between today and the death of the organism, and so express its date.

So far, so good. Radiocarbon dating has often been described as a godsend to archaeologists, but like all such gifts it has to be

3

treated circumspectly and with understanding. In the first place the basic physics involved means that the 'date' can be expressed only as a statistical statement of probability, usually a single standard deviation (a 66 per cent chance of the date lying between two extremes). The second limitation, which stems from the comparatively short half-life, is that dates beyond about 50,000 years ago cannot at present be obtained by the method: by then the radiocarbon remnant is so tiny as to be almost imperceptible. A last factor is more immediately significant for us in this book. The principle of C-14 dating was set out by 1950, but within a decade or so tests against ancient historically dated samples showed discrepancies, so a further series of tests were made against the count of the annual growth-rings of trees, especially a species of fantastically slow-growing American pine, enabling a tree-ring chronology going back some 8,000 years to be made. When radiocarbon dates were determined from a series of tree-ring dated samples of wood, it was found that the former departed from the latter in an irregular but constant curve as one went back in time, showing that radiocarbon 'years' were not equivalent to calendar years, but gave consistently 'younger' readings. As an instance, the radiocarbon dates of about 2500–2000 bc for the occupation of Skara Brae in Orkney should read something like 3100–2450 BC in our normal calendar chronology. For uniformity in this book, which also uses dates historically computed, the radiocarbon dates have been brought into line by the appropriate conversions which are now possible.

We are part of the Northern World: the Orkneys are nearer to the Arctic Circle than to Oxford, and Ben Nevis is equidistant from Paris and from Iceland. The western sea-ways linked the cold and misty north to the sunny civilising south, so that from the fourth millennium BC onwards there was trafficking, and a coming and going of peoples, between Europe and west Britain and Ireland, voyaging that continues into history with the travels of the Celtic saints and scholars, and the wine trade from the Loire and Garonne. Across the North Sea, trade and sea movements linked Britain with the Low Countries and the North European plain, with those regions where the merchants of the Hanseatic League were later to build up and develop trade connections which themselves go back to prehistoric antiquity. By land-routes over the Border passes, but even more by the activities of coasting craft, the ebb and flow of contacts between the north and south of Britain was maintained, and through south Britain across the Channel to the Continent.

We have to reckon with innovation and conservatism, change and stagnation, adaptation and absorption. New peoples, with new ideas and new techniques, arrive in Scotland, and their settlement and diffusion are almost inevitably determined by such natural factors as harbours, forests or rivers. Once established, their traditions take on a distinctively insular form, whether they developed in isolation from outside connections or evolved as a result of give-and-take with other communities. At the dawn of history, we seem to see an equally intriguing amalgam of new and old in prehistory, contributing to the make-up of the Picts.

Inescapably, the physical geography of Scotland confronts us, in exaggerated and often dramatic form, with highland and lowland in antithesis, and to the Highlands belongs the sea-divided, sea-linked world of the Islands. Indeed the pattern of ancient human settlement shows that, as a result of the tide-races and inhospitable shores of the stormy seas between the Hebrides and the mainland, the prehistoric population of the western Highlands was strung out along the Atlantic coasts of the Western Isles rather than on that of the mainland; eastwards across the Minch and over to the Great Glen were the virtually uninhabited barren lands. On the physical map of Scotland, the mountain massif of the Highlands dominates the north and west of the country in size and bulk, but throughout antiquity it was, at most, a region of passage, very largely uninhabited and with such scanty population as it possessed to be found along the natural lines of communication which linked the more favoured areas where agriculture and pasturage could form an assured basis for the life of settled communities. Apart from these routes through the mountains, to which we will return, human settlement of the Scottish Highlands was in certain areas on the coastal fringes, as in Caithness and

Sutherland (but hardly at all on the west from Cape Wrath to Fort William), in the Western Isles, Orkney and Shetland, and in the glens opening out on to the north-eastern coastal plain which stretches from Stirling to the Moray Firth. This latter region, together with the Midland Valley and what are technically the Southern Uplands, formed the major area of settlement of ancient as of modern Scotland. Definitions of what constitute 'The Highlands' are various, and anything but precise: here they will be taken in their most reasonable, geographical sense, to denote the Highland mountain massif above about 230 m to 300 m, but to include the related, if orographically unqualified, regions north of the Moray Firth.

The key to almost all movement into and from Scotland is the sea coast, land communications with northern England being confined to a few passes from the Cheviot massif, and routes along the coastal plain to east and west of this: here coasting traffic would in fact be as good or better as a means of travel. Movement by water, whether on sea or lake or by river, has great advantages for primitive or simple communities using small shallow-draught vessels, especially in the transport of relatively bulky or heavy goods in the absence of suitable pack-animals other than men themselves. Throughout prehistory we find that the rivers formed the routes which linked the coast to the hinterland and indeed formed natural highways across country. The deeply indented coastline of Scotland, with estuaries and sea lochs penetrating deeply into the land mass, and with freshwater lochs linked by rivers strung out along the Highland glens, made water communications possible from sea to sea with a minimum of portages overland. Furthermore, by the adroit use of such routes, it was often possible to avoid tricky seas around headland and promontory and to make that kind of transpeninsular travel which was familiar throughout the ancient world and is reflected in the Odyssey and the voyage of the Argonauts.

There is no direct evidence in Britain for the use of plank-built boats until later prehistoric times around 1650 BC (though they may have existed at earlier periods). River traffic at all events would have involved either dug-out canoes, made by hollowing out a half log, or light skin-covered craft of the type of curraghs and coracles: the latter were used on the Spey until recent times.

In Scotland the most remarkable and obvious example of such a transpeninsular route is that afforded by the Great Glen, linking the Atlantic coasts to those of the North Sea and cutting diagonally from south-west to north-east through the heart of the Highland massif. Traffic along this route would avoid the necessity of rounding Cape Wrath and of going through the Pentland Firth. Indeed, the lack of any extensive prehistoric settlement on the mainland coast north of Ardna-murchan may in no small measure be a reflection of the tend-ency for northward-bound craft to use this route, rather than to coast along the picturesque but inhospitable western shore. A minor transpeninsular route seems to have existed between Thurso and Wick, along the lines of rivers giving their names to those Caithness towns, a route which likewise avoided the perils of the Pentland Firth. Alternative routes from west to east could also be followed, as for instance that from Loch Linnhe at the south-western end of the Glen, by Glen Spean and Loch Laggan to the valley of the Spey, and, farther south, less well-defined routes through more difficult country to Loch Tay and Loch Earn, and so leading to the estuaries of the Tay and Forth. The Clyde and Forth estuaries themselves of course form a notable transpeninsular route, although in fact there is little evidence of its use in antiquity. In the Lowlands, the Tweed and its tributaries penetrate deeply into the hill country between the Cheviots and the Lammermuirs. In the south-west again, an important route ran across Argyll from Crinan Loch to Lochgilphead on the line of what was to be-come the Crinan Canal, thus avoiding the detour and the heavy seas incident to rounding the Mull of Kintyre.

We must not, of course, picture these valley routes as they appear to us today, running clear and for the most part through open country. The artificial and man-made quality of almost all British (indeed of almost all European) landscape is fre-quently forgotten, but must constantly be remembered in any study of human settlement in the past. The natural condition of northern Europe is forest, inhibited only by altitude, thin-ness of soil, climatic extremes of cold or wet or wind, or by the

presence of fresh-water or salt marshland: in Scotland (as in Britain as a whole) the natural tree-line for most of prehistoric and all of historic times, would have approximated to the 300 m contour and exceptionally would have reached 450 m or even 600 m. Below this, save in exposed situations, the natural state of vegetation – the botanical climax reached without interference – would be forest of some kind. We shall see something of the sequence of British forest history in remote antiquity later on, but we can note now that, from the period of man's first inhabiting Scotland into the present time, the characteristic woodland of the Lowlands is the mixed oak forest dominated by oak, ash and elm (but not including in earlier times beech, a relatively recent addition to British forest trees). Farther north, while the mixed oak-woods continue in favoured valley situations, the more upland forest growth is the hardier birch, rowan and pine, at times sparse and scattered.

Natural oak-woods may still exist, for instance, in the Great Glen, Glen Garry and at Craigendarroch in the Dee valley, and the native pine forest survives in such places as the Black Wood of Rannoch, Ballochbuie Forest and at Rothiemurchus. Birch-woods are of course widespread, and climatically the Highland birch- and pine-woods are relics of the south-westward extension of the North European coniferous forest, bounded on the south by the summer deciduous forest of mixed oak type.

Of course the rivers would not afford the only natural routes of communication: ridge-routes over the more open hill country would have existed, or cross-country tracks through the forest, especially where well-drained ground came down to the river's edge. These routes would have been traversed on foot until the later prehistoric periods, when pack animals may have been employed. There is no good evidence for wheeled transport in Britain before about the eighth century B C at the earliest, though there is some evidence for the use of sledges at a considerably earlier date – after all, these are still useful pieces of equipment on hill farms today.

Ancient Scotland, then, would have been a land of forests, through which the rivers ran their irregular courses, straggling here in slow streams through swamps grown thick with alder and willow, there dammed and temporarily diverted by fallen trees and accumulated vegetation brought down by the winter floods. Nevertheless they must have formed a recognisable, moving highway along the heavily overgrown valley, above which towered the higher hills, barren and forbidding above the tree-line, and offering no attraction to farmer or herdsman. The constantly recurrent motif of antiquity is that of forest clearance; throughout Scottish prehistory echoes the sound of the woodman's axe, its blade of stone, flint, bronze, iron. Into the forests there penetrated pioneers with felling-axes, farmers with new land to clear and plant, traders anxious to push their way up new rivers in adventurous canoes, and meeting the trappers with a wary eye on the bows and arrows. If we think of the early European settlers in North America and Canada we shall have taken a step in visualising our first agricultural colonists making their way into Britain in the fourth millennium BC. Lightly wooded but potentially fertile land would be at a premium with the early colonists, especially when it lay near to suitable beaches or natural routes of inland communication. If the distribution of prehistoric settlement is compared with the soil classification on the maps of the Land Utilisation Survey, one sees how ancient and modern agriculture are alike controlled by the natural suitability of the soil for cultivation by digging-stick, hoe or plough, and how the waste lands of today were those of prehistory also; the proximity of modern croft to ancient broch and chambered cairn, can also often show on a smaller scale how good land once found will be recognised as such for six thousand years.

It is only to be expected that the wild fauna of prehistoric Scotland should have been more abundant and varied than it is today. The forests were the habitat of the red deer, a woodland animal considerably larger in antiquity than today, for its modern descendants are stunted in size from inadequate conditions for feeding. There, too, lived the roe deer and the wild boar, and extinct wild cattle (the so-called 'wild' herds such as Cadzow or Chillingham must be descendants of domesticated forms). The brown bear was known even from southern England in the second millennium BC, and survived long in Wales and Scotland; so, too, beavers, wolverines (the skins of which were used for a cloak for the Duke of Northumberland's cousin in 1556), and wolves: a well-known fourteenth-century map of Britain marks *Hic habundant lupi* – here wolves abound – in north-west Sutherland. Saga references imply that even reindeer survived in Caithness until Viking times. Among the birds, the most famous species then found and now extinct is the great auk. Other birds were then common which now are but visitors to these shores, such as cranes. And in addition there were then as now grouse, black-cock, and capercailzie.

With the possible exception of the pig, which could have been domesticated locally in Britain as elsewhere in northern Europe, and probably too the dog, all the farmyard animals which we encounter in Scottish prehistory – cattle, sheep, goats, horses – must have been introduced from the Continent to Britain as already tamed and modified species. Indeed, it is almost certain that all the domestic animals (except the horse) were introduced together into Britain before 4000 BC. So too the grain – wheat or barley, and much later oats and rye – would have been brought with the agricultural immigrants when they first arrived from Europe.

It is against this natural background of a land slowly being won from nature by successive generations of farmers and stockbreeders, and with its communications being opened up and its natural resources exploited by traders and craftsmen, that we must set the story of prehistoric Scotland. At all times there was enough and to spare for those who were prepared to take on the task; at all times the population, by any modern industrialised standards, was tiny and widely scattered, the opportunities for expansion and fresh settlement unlimited. New immigrations could be, and were, imperceptibly absorbed; new overlordships were accepted or imposed. Despite its geographical remoteness, Scotland was at no time wholly unaffected by the major developments in technology originating in or transmitted to Britain and the European continent. Nor was it uninfluenced by the movements of people affecting those regions. Ancient society outside the Oriental and Classical World was essentially fluid and mobile, with an economic structure more primitive and less stabilised than that centred on the city and the city-state. We have to reckon with a stage of affairs when even agricultural communities may shift their territories as they temporarily exhaust the land, and among these more stable economies there were still more mobile pastoralists and people with long-surviving traditions of living by hunting and food-gathering. Historians thinking only in terms of the stable economies of mediaeval and modern Europe, noted with surprise the time of folk-movements, following the collapse of the Roman Empire, and named them the Migration Period, but this was no more than a return to the conditions of prehistoric Europe, which had been forced into temporary immobility by Roman rule. A Europe of permanently settled agricultural and urban mercantile communities was an achievement of the Middle Ages, and for an historical counterpart to the conditions of prehistory we must look to the period of the Saxon settlements, the raids of the Norsemen on these islands and the movements of Goth, Vandal and Burgundian on the Continent.

Primitive or simple societies of agriculturalists and pastoralists are the subject matter of Scottish prehistory. The technological skill of these people, once they had mastered the use of metals, differed in degree rather than in kind from that of early mediaeval Europe. Their social systems varied, shall we say, from that of the Polynesians or of the Maoris as encountered by Captain Cook to that reflected in Homer or the Cuchulainn stories, and they formed a sparse and at times probably a relatively mobile population in a heavily wooded northern country. Except in the latest stages of the story they are in the strict sense prehistoric: anonymous peoples whose languages are unknown and of whom a restricted and one-sided knowledge has been obtained by archaeological means alone in default of any historical record.

Archaeology comprises a constantly elaborating set of techniques for obtaining knowledge of communities by means other than the use of written records. For periods or regions where such historical records exist, archaeology can amplify and extend the knowledge these provide. But of extinct communities for which no written record, direct or indirect, exists, and which are therefore non-historic or prehistoric, archaeological techniques alone can recover knowledge, and inference from archaeological evidence constitutes prehistory. Indeed, the existence of the communities we describe, their movements, trade and contacts, are themselves inferences from the material objects which have survived to be studied by the process of archaeology. Some understanding of the nature of these processes and more particularly an appreciation of their limitations is necessary to assess the peculiar quality of prehistory and its relation to historical method.

The reconstruction of prehistory by means of archaeology involves, as we have just seen, a series of inferences from material evidence which consists of the accidentally surviving remnants of the objects made and used, or of the structures built, by peoples in the past. An historical record is something deliberately recorded with a view to its transmission to a future reader, whether a week or a century later. This does not mean, of course, that the information extracted by an historian from a document is necessarily the information its compiler intended to transmit, but nevertheless an original intention to put something on record is implied. Archaeological evidence, on the other hand, is accidental evidence: no-one made pots or built a broch with an eye to posterity. But a study of the distribution of distinctive pottery styles can lead to inferences about the affinities and movements of their makers; the planning and construction of a broch can indicate the likely sources of the architectural traditions of its builders. It will be realised that, in the interpretation of archaeological evidence, there are many pitfalls and difficulties, and one arises from what may be called the accident of survival. The normal processes of decay result in the bulk of the material used as archaeological evidence being of resistant substances, such as stone or metal, less frequently bone or antler, and only in exceptional circumstances such perishable materials as wood, leather, fabric, netting or ropes. Occasionally inference at a second stage can be used, as when the plan of a timber building may be recovered from the post-holes dug to hold its uprights even when no wood survives, but on the whole we tend to find ourselves in a situation where we have fairly complete evidence on, for instance, the types and processes of manufacture of bronze axe-blades or spear heads, but with very little knowledge of their wooden hafts or shafts, and none whatever of the clothing of the people who made and used them. This then is a limitation always to be borne in mind: prehistoric man's equipment and possessions were far more elaborate and varied than the relatively imperishable fragments in our museums or in the countryside would at first sight suggest.

There is a second point not perhaps so immediately apparent, but of the highest importance in understanding the nature of archaeological evidence. This evidence, as we have seen, consists of the surviving remnants of what man has made – his material culture, in archaeological terms. It follows then that the information it can give us will be very largely technological: what types of tools or weapons or pots, what kind of houses or tombs were built by this or that prehistoric community, and in what regions. Study of the food refuse (animal bones, charred grain or its impressions accidentally preserved on pottery) will contribute, with the more specifically man-made material, evidence for the type of economy – hunter, pastoralist, agriculturalist – of the settlement we are studying and whose plan we can recover by excavation. So we can say something about subsistence and trade, about primitive economics in fact, in addition to our knowledge of the community's technology (whether they used bronze, or drove a horse and cart).

But when we try to go further we get into difficulties. Something can be deduced or surmised of social organisation, partly by more recent or historical analogies, but here one is beginning to force archaeological evidence to the extreme of its limits. Tombs may tell us that collective or individual burial, inhumation or cremation, were prescribed by the religious canons of the particular community, but there is no means of knowing what set of beliefs was really involved. Some of the most striking prehistoric monuments in Scotland are the great stone-chambered collective tombs such as Maes Howe in Orkney – we can recognise in their formal traditions of ritual architecture connections with other regions of western Europe, but can say no more of the religion of which they are the tangible expression than we could of Christianity or Islam had all historical records perished and we set about reconstructing their beliefs and rituals from a study of churches and mosques long deserted and ruined. And language, that essential and evanescent medium for creating and transmitting all ideas and traditions – here archaeological evidence in itself must of its very nature fail us completely. Earlier prehistory in Europe is anonymous and silent until languages are recorded by writing or are among those surviving to the present day. Calgacus is the first inhabitant of Scotland we know by name, the Celtic languages the first we can surely recognise, at the dawn of history, and even though other earlier tongues can be inferred, we cannot understand them or assess their affinities, nor will archaeology by itself help us.

We must remember, in fact, that archaeological evidence, like any other, can only give answers to questions framed with an appreciation of its potentialities and its limitations. It will tell us much about an individual's or a group's technological achievements, their regions of settlement, and something of at least the less perishable objects of trade or barter: it can establish their chronological position in the local or wider sequence. It will not inform us on the language or religion involved, nor the social organisation, except by inference and analogy. In the course of this book it will become apparent how often we must confess ignorance in prehistory. But nevertheless, we have achieved a great deal in extending the historical perspective far beyond the earliest date possible by the use of written records, and however incomplete the picture of prehistory afforded by archaeological means, it is better than no picture at all. We cannot ignore the prehistory behind history, and it has content enough to form a significant contribution to our knowledge of the past.

II

The natural conditions of the Scottish landscape which we
have just described must be reckoned 'modern' by the standards of geologists or botanists: the climatic conditions which
ultimately controlled it were established some 10,000 years
ago, and with relatively minor fluctuations have continued to
the present day. The fourth of the great geological epochs, the
Quaternary Period, was for the northern hemisphere a time of
great climatic extremes, and arctic conditions alternated with
those of the comparative warmth of modern temperate Europe.
These glacial and inter-glacial periods, the causes of which are
imperfectly known, though changes in solar radiation doubtless played an important part, culminated in a final glaciation
in which the southern edge of the permanent arctic ice-cap at
its maximum crossed the English midlands; southwards – the
Channel not then formed – a strip of what is now England was
then the northernmost habitable fringe of western Europe, a
barren tundra beyond which stretched the desolation of the
ice-sheet.

At this time – and if we want a date, twenty thousand years

ago would be a fair estimate – man was already an old-established inhabitant of Europe, man modern in all physical characteristics, a fire-maker and a skilled craftsman in stone, bone and wood, a hunter dependent for food and clothing on the animals with which he shared the arctic environment, and with whose migratory movements his own existence was closely interwoven. Following the herds of reindeer that were his main quarry as they moved over the tundra, his winter quarters alone could be semi-permanent, and where the limestone provided natural protection in rock shelters and caves, the little family groups could return seasonally and stand the siege of winter. Man was a rare animal, and it has been reasonably estimated that in the habitable areas of what is now southern England, as far north as Derbyshire and even, late on in the last glaciation, west Yorkshire, the total population need not have been more than 250 persons in the final phase of the Old Stone Age, or Upper Palaeolithic period.

The inexorable swing of climatic change brought an extension of habitable land as, slowly and imperceptibly, so that no one generation could see the difference, the ice-sheet, melting each summer at its southern fringe, retreated northwards. By about ten thousand years ago this retreat was bringing the arctic but habitable zone northwards towards Scotland and southern Scandinavia. The process continued, wavering as temperatures dropped a few degrees in the annual average, and the glaciers once again pushed their way down valleys they had themselves carved out, but there was no major re-advance of the ice-sheet. The post-glacial phase in which we find ourselves today had established itself.

But we are dealing with natural processes which in terms of the fleeting human generations seem of immeasurable slowness. The changing climatic conditions after the last ice age, and the consequent variations in the North European plant life by which they can in the main be detected, are spread out over ten millennia, and so far as Scotland is concerned, man hardly appears in the landscape before modern conditions are being established. The determination of these vegetational changes has been due to the combined work of botanists and geologists, and its mainstay has been the fact that the pollen-grains of plants are not only distinguishable, one species from another, to the trained eye with a microscope, but that they are far more resistant to decay than the remainder of the vegetable organism. Pollen is airborne, and at the varying flowering seasons of trees and other plants a 'pollen-rain', as it is called, is continuously falling, and drifting with the wind. On pools and lakes where peat is forming, the pollen is held by the surface attraction of the water, and falls to form a resistant component of the peat-bed. As the vegetation changes in response to alterations in climate (or, when man deliberately upsets the balance of plant life by forest clearance or the cultivation of land), so the proportion of species in the pollen-rain will alter, and the peat-bogs, building up insensibly a stratified sequence, will preserve in their layers a record of the changing vegetation of the region which may extend over many thousand years. By the technique of pollen-analysis, therefore, the vegetational history of northern Europe has been built up, aided of course by actual plant remains, such as leaves or seeds, where these survive in favoured circumstances.

In what are technically known as Late-Glacial times the North European plain, south Scandinavia and much of the British Isles had a vegetation of sub-arctic tundra type, of which that charming flower the mountain avens (*Dryas octopetala*) is so distinctive as to give its name to this Dryas Period. The period is in fact divided into two by an interval of warmer climate, with a consequent great increase of luxuriant grassland, notable in the British Isles as being the period in which flourished that noble extinct animal, the giant Irish deer, owing to the good grazing that the grasslands of the time afforded. Deposits of this phase have been identified in Scotland, where, as elsewhere, they can be dated to the span of about 12,000 to 11,000 years ago.

The sequence continues with progressive amelioration of the climate and with the beginnings of the change-over, made possible by this tempering of conditions, from open tundra to forest. The earliest colonists are the birch trees, followed soon by pine as the dominant forest cover, through the pre-Boreal and Boreal phases (about 10,000 to 7,000 years ago). Then, warmer and moister conditions make possible the dominance,

YEARS	CULTURE	CLIMATE	CLIMATIC CHANGE	TREES	ERA
2000					
1000					
AD BC	Iron				
1000	Bronze	sub-Atlantic	rapid deterioration		POST-GLACIAL
2000		sub-Boreal		elm / alder	
3000	Neolithic		climatic optimum	mixed oak	
4000		Atlantic			
5000					
6000	Mesolithic	Boreal	rapid warming	hazel	
7000		pre-Boreal		pine	
8000					
9000	Upper Palaeolithic	Upper Dryas	cold	birch	LATE GLACIAL
10000			milder		
11000		Lower Dryas	cold		
12000					

even in northern Scotland, of the mixed-oak forest of the type
familiar today throughout temperate Europe, where human
activity has not altered the natural balance of vegetation. This,
the Atlantic phase, is followed by the somewhat drier sub-
Boreal, of great significance to Britain in that it sees the arrival
in these islands of the first agriculturalists, immigrants from
the European continent, which had been severed from the
British Isles by the formation, in the Boreal phase, about 6500
B C, of the English Channel.

These changes in the landscape, and especially the growth of
forests, meant of course a corresponding change in the animal
population. The reindeer moved north with the tundra, which
is their natural habitat, to the sub-arctic zone where they still
survive. The hunters of the Upper Palaeolithic age were faced
with a choice no less important from its being unconscious
and unapprehended: to move ever northwards with the animals to which their livelihood was so intimately bound, or to
adapt themselves to changing conditions of environment and
food supply. Such changes had indeed been made millennia
before, as the warm inter-glacial periods had been succeeded
by the onset of colder conditions, and temperate flora and
fauna had been replaced by those habituated to low temperatures. But for northern Europe the final retreat of the ice-sheet
marks a decisive moment in which the foundations of much of
later prehistory were laid, for the adaptive qualities of mankind enabled adjustments to be made to a wholly changed
natural environment. This period marks the beginnings of
man's control of nature rather than his passive acceptance of
it; a control at first unconscious but soon to become deliberate
and of increasing strength.

To this phase of response to the challenge of changing environment, with its resultant modifications of technology, the
name of the Mesolithic Period was given by archaeologists – a
Middle Stone Age in the older conception of epochs differen-
tiated by the standard material (stone, bronze, iron) used for
edge-tools, intermediate between the Old and the New Stone
Ages, the Palaeolithic and the Neolithic Periods. Some now
tend to regard the changes in basic economy – from hunting
and food-gathering to agriculture and stock-breeding – as more

21

significant criteria, but even from this standpoint the Mesolithic Period in northern Europe with its hunting and fishing
economy can better be seen as a prelude in man's command of
his environment which could readily accommodate such
novel techniques as those of the farmer, introduced from outside. In western Asia, where stock-breeding and agriculture
began, it was among Mesolithic communities that these basic
revolutions in human livelihood took place, and even in northern Europe and Britain we shall see how the old hunter-fisher
traditions may have contributed not a little to the pattern of
life in later prehistoric times. Indeed in Scotland, as in the
other countries on the northern rim of the Old World, we see
how strong in these regions was the force of survival of techniques and economies devised to exploit an environment in
which agriculture could at best obtain an insecure and un-
happy footing.

Up to the time of the formation of the English Channel and
the concurrent extension of the North Sea to approximately its
present shores, England, at least as far north as east Yorkshire,
formed the western edge of the North European plain, populated (doubtless still thinly) by communities of Mesolithic
culture having common traditions in their technology and
their economy of existence. The pine forests of Boreal times
prevented extensive settlement except by rivers and lakes and
on the coasts; to hunting and food-gathering, fishing formed
an increasingly important adjunct. But the attack on the forests had begun, and a tool unknown to earlier times was
invented, the woodman's axe, with its blade of flaked flint.
The challenge of artificial transport was met by the contrivance of boats, of hollowed tree trunks, or of a skin-covered
wooden framework; to cross the winter snows in more open
areas sledges and skis were devised. No mean inventions these,
the axe, the boat and the sledge, to hand down to posterity.

In north-east Yorkshire we know of the existence of such
communities in early Boreal times, with a date of about 8500
BC. Our story of the beginnings of Scotland as a region of
human settlement opens then about nine thousand years ago.
We know of these people from two main regions: one on the
west, near Oban, and in islands such as Jura and Risga, and

22

Oronsay by Colonsay, and as far south as Kirkcudbrightshire; the other in the estuary of the Forth in the Stirling region. Scattered finds suggest at least hunting parties if not settlements in Banffshire, the Fife coast, the Tweed basin and Ayrshire. There must have been very few of these people, widely scattered and seasonally migrant overland or by boat along the coasts. Self-sufficient though such communities were, they had one need in essential raw materials that could not be adequately or easily satisfied, and that was a sufficient supply of flints for their tools, and for arming weapons such as arrows. We shall see how the need for tough stones for axe-blades in rather later prehistoric times led to something approaching a systematic trade between areas of supply and demand, and no doubt even beach-pebble flint was a valuable commodity to the Mesolithic people.

Even though they probably reached Scotland largely as the result of land journeys over the southern part of what is now the North Sea, and from the more southerly parts of Britain, these colonists were people of the coasts, well accustomed to movement by sea and river. The Mesolithic settlements on islands such as Oronsay or Risga make it clear that boats of some sort were in common use. The dug-out canoe was a type which persisted throughout prehistory, and such craft were still in use as ferries in the Highlands in the eighteenth century. There is some inferential evidence that northern people at this time could also have used skin-covered boats of the type of the Eskimo umiak.

The west coast settlements are marked by the huge accumulated middens of discarded shells of over two dozen species of mollusc, including limpets, mussels, whelks and oysters, testifying to innumerable successive meals of sea-food in seasonal camps at the same spot. The diet of these people included, too, fish such as saithe, conger, bream, wrasse, haddock and dogfish, and meat of wild boar and red deer. Some of these fish are what are known as bottom-feeders in the ocean, and can only be caught by line-fishing from a boat. That as well as lines, these people used basket-work lobster-pots too, is by no means unlikely. They hunted probably with bows and arrows, and certainly with spears and harpoons armed with barbed points

23

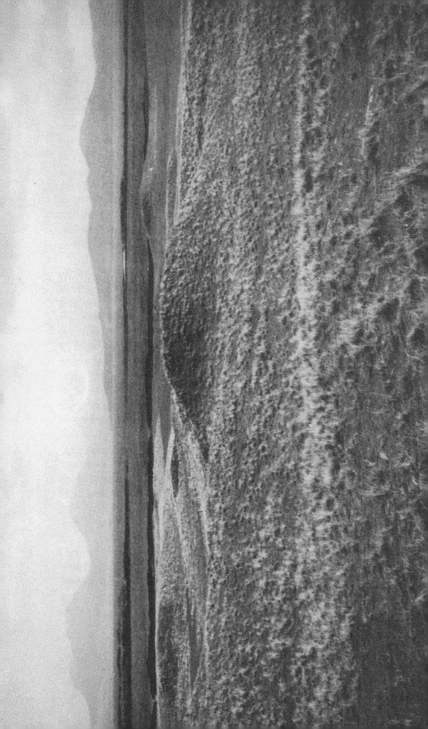

cut from deer antler. These spears could be used either for fish or seals, or for hunting on land. Seals were hunted and must have been a valuable source of skins and furs, and even if live whales were not harpooned, their stranded carcasses were certainly appreciated as a means of obtaining meat, blubber and oil in quantity.

Finds in the Forth estuary give us a fascinating view of such activities. In the fifth millennium BC, what are now the flat lands of the Carse of Stirling were shallow tidal areas of mud which were evidently deathtraps to whales that were caught by the ebbing tides. Skeletons of such stranded beasts have been dug from these clay beds, and with one at Meiklewood was found an implement of antler, bored through to take a wooden haft, and having a cutting edge like the Eskimo tools which are used to hack whale blubber. A great vertebra of a whale from the same clay had its flat surface criss-crossed by cuts, thus showing it to have been used as a chopping-block. Other mattocks, usually in fragments broken at the shaft-hole, come from the west coast sites, and we have a vivid glimpse of the earliest inhabitants of Scotland eagerly taking advantage of the good luck afforded by a stranding. Wild fowl were also eaten, for the bones of the extinct great auk, cormorants, gulls, gannets and guillemots have been found in the middens. They may have been trapped or shot by bow and arrow, or even caught by flinging a contraption of weighted strings into a low-flying flock, as is done among Eskimo communities. Feathers were probably used as arrow flights or for adornment, and vanity was also served by making necklaces of shells. Clothing must have been of skins and furs, and though we have no direct evidence, it is likely that the making of adequate skin garments, cut and sewn with sinews, may well go back to a remote period of prehistory, even into the later Palaeolithic. The tailored garment, in fact, and the use of trousers as a warm leg covering, are likely to be contributions to our comfort from the Mesolithic north, rather than from what were to become the centres of ancient civilisation in more southern and warmer regions, where the early invention of woven cloth gave rise

Oronsay, with Jura in background

to the simpler hot-weather clothing of the type of toga, burnous, dhoti and sarong.

Left to themselves, the Mesolithic inhabitants of Britain and
of northern Europe, having once made a satisfactory adaptation of their way of life in response to their environment, could
hardly have made many significant developments in technology beyond those already mastered. Much of the area in
which Mesolithic tradition survived was an area of conservatism in which no incentive presented itself to alter a long-estab-
lished economy which, after all, had the great merit of func-
tioning efficiently within the limitations imposed by environment and a technology based on locally available materials.
The domestication of the dog had been achieved by the Mesolithic peoples. In the forest areas the potentialities of a rudimentary taming of pigs could have been realised independent-
ly of any introduction of novel ideas from outside. But in
default of suitable wild species of animals or plants, the domestication of cattle, sheep or goats, and the cultivation of
grain, was an impossibility in northern Europe. The wild ancestors of our farmyard stock and of our cereal crops were to be
found only in a belt of country centred in western Asia, where a
climate more genial than that of northern Europe favoured the
development of the earliest farming communities.

Agriculture, then, with the changed pattern of life it imposed
on hunting and food-gathering peoples, could only have become established in Britain as the result of actual immigrations of farming communities, who brought with them not
only the abstract knowledge of agricultural techniques, but the
practical means, in the form of seed corn and young stock, of
setting up a farm in new territory. Across the European continent the earliest stone-using farming communities had spread,
by land along great rivers like the Danube and by coasting
voyages westwards along the Mediterranean shores. Such communities were established in Western Europe before 4500 BC
and, within a century or two, the earliest landings in southern
and eastern England must have taken place across the narrows
of the Channel. Western England, south Wales and Ireland
were probably receiving similar immigrants by coasting move-

ments or from points farther west along the European seaboard at much the same time. The new agricultural economy introduced by these settlers was mixed farming. They raised a cereal crop, mainly wheat, but with some barley, and they kept domesticated cattle, sheep, goats, pigs and dogs. They lived in settlements comprising stone or timber-built dwellings and enclosures, and they knew the craft of pot-making. Hunters or nomads have little use for pots and pans of baked clay, cumbersome, heavy and fragile; for them skin, leather, wood or basketry provide the necessary containers. But in the farmstead or village pots are important for storage, cooking and drinking. Easily broken but hardly less easily replaced, durable in fragments, localised and conservative in form and pattern, these pots provide the archaeologist with an invaluable clue to the distribution and inter-relations of prehistoric communities. Much of this book is built (we trust fairly securely) on a foundation of potsherds.

In the old standard terminology these first farmers represent the Neolithic Period, the New Stone Age. But it was not only new in those modifications of stone-working techniques on which the nomenclature was originally based, it was an innovation in living technique. The spread of farming communities between 5000 and 3000 BC linked the barbarians of the European continent to the developing civilisations of the Ancient East by a common pattern of life which, however much it differed in degree, shared the basic elements of agricultural economies with the settled life and technological developments they implied. More than that, it laid the foundations of mediaeval and modern Europe.

It is difficult to estimate the length of time it may have taken before farming communities settled in Scotland after the first establishment of the colonies in southern England or Ireland. In prehistory as in history one can never infer uniformity in the absence of direct evidence, and new people and their techniques may travel slowly or fast from one region to another. A little flotilla of boats could have put out from east Yorkshire and coasted up to Aberdeenshire in a single fine spell of summer weather; it could be a matter of several generations before the shift of population brought colonists to the Clyde. Rarely can one distinguish by archaeological evidence the hares from the tortoises in the movements of peoples or the indirect transmission of ideas.

Within whatever time-span it may have been, and on the whole the evidence favours quick movement, agricultural communities were establishing themselves in Scotland along more than one route. Up the east coast, at least as far as the Moray Firth, there is evidence of settlements and tombs likely to have had connections with communities in Yorkshire, with whom they shared some pottery styles and the custom of burial under long earthen mounds (long barrows) or, less often, long cairns of stones. Wherever they settled, their immediate problem was that of forest clearance, to secure patches of land for cultivation by digging-stick, hoe, or simple plough of *ard* type, and to find grazing on herbage or tree foliage for their flocks and herds. Axe-blades, flaked and ground from flint or tough rocks, were in constant demand; the trees once roughly felled, clearance by burning could proceed, and the ground between the stumps, enriched by ash, could be hacked up and planted with seed corn. Near Montrose the long barrow of Dalladies was built of turf from recently fire-cleared land about 3400 BC.

This demand for stone axe-blades was met in more than one way. In south and south-east England flint was mined from the chalk, and the occasional fine flint axes from Scotland may well be imports from English axe-factories, or have been brought by the early colonists from east Yorkshire. Suitable rocks for axes would of course be recognised in many regions, and pebbles or lumps from the screes ground to shape on the spot. But really good tough stones which will take and maintain a workmanlike cutting edge are not to be found everywhere, and before long the outstanding properties of certain rocks were recognised, and at times their outcrops were systematically exploited in regular factories whose exports were spread far and wide. In Scotland, localised production at least took place at outcrops near Killin in Perthshire and again in Shetland.

Stone axe with wooden haft, from Isle of Lewis

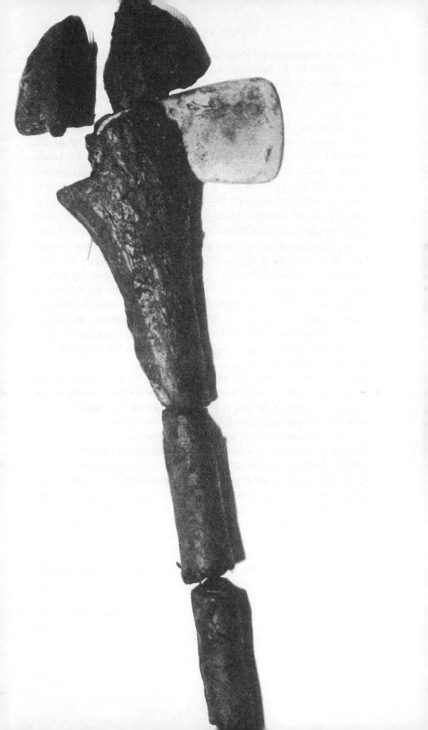

The recognition of this industry and widespread trade in Neolithic Britain has been one of the major developments in the archaeology of this period. The means by which it has been achieved, though simple in theory, is laborious in practice, involving the co-operation of archaeologists and geologists and the cutting of thin sections from all available stone axe-heads for examination under the petrological microscope. The results, slowly accumulating and still mounting up, have been mildly spectacular. Of the major centres of axe-production which have been identified, three supplied axes to very distant areas, including Scotland. The one in north Wales is of minor importance for us. But the axes from Great Langdale in the Lake District and Tievebulliagh Hill in Antrim seem to have been particularly acceptable to the Scottish market. Pottery types as well as axes suggest that not only trade but colonisation also was effected from Ulster to Aberdeenshire and east Scotland generally. The axes from Great Langdale found in the Lowlands, and occasionally as far afield as the Hebrides, suggest extensive trade, as does their remarkable concentration around the Humber in England. Of course we do not know by what primitive means of exchange this trade was carried on, nor what commodities were bartered for the axes, by the Scottish Neolithic settlers. Archaeology, as we have seen, can only detect the durable objects surviving from the past, and primitive scales of values are not ours: who knows but that an eagle's tail feathers, a wild cat's pelt or even a handful of sea-shells endowed with magic properties may have been considered an adequate price for a Tievebulliagh axe-head?

We must reckon too with the exchange of presents, as between chieftains, or the giving of gifts by traders in earnest of good faith and in lively anticipation of favours to come. Indeed, an axe-blade need not even be utilitarian, but if sufficiently splendid, it may take on a symbolic meaning and become an object, or weapon, of prestige. We shall come across such objects more than once in Scottish prehistory, and in the Neolithic period they are surely represented by the superb axe-blades of highly polished jadeite (from the Continent), glassy and undamaged, some of which have been found in Scotland, and more elsewhere in the British Isles. Objects of prestige are with us today, as fur coats or expensive cars; perhaps more comparable with the useless jadeite axe-blades are diamonds, or the bars of gold in our national vaults, which we endow with unreal and talismanic values.

The settlements of the earliest Scottish farmers, as elsewhere in the British Isles, have left us little to recognise on the surface. The post-holes of timber-framed houses, and their hearths, can be recovered by excavation only if chance discoveries lead us to the spot. At Rothesay, in Bute, a fragment of a Neolithic settlement, accidentally dug into by a sandpit, produced not only pottery and the post-holes of walling or fencing, but charred wheat grains as well. Paradoxically enough, the most striking remains of Neolithic settlements in Britain are to be found in the most unsuitable areas for primitive farming, in Orkney and in Shetland. We must remember this remote geographical setting when considering the sites in question. They represent individual and insular adaptations to extraordinary circumstances of climate and terrain. We would be wrong if, because Skara Brae shows (as it does) Stone Age architecture in astonishing detail, and a state of preservation unparalleled in contemporary northern Europe, we then went on to generalise from it and regard it as typical of Britain or even of the rest of Scotland at that time.

Our knowledge of vegetation in Orkney and Shetland in the third millennium BC indicates a generally treeless landscape dominated by birch and hazel shrubland and heath. At Skara Brae on Mainland, and at Rinyo on Rousay, settlements consisting of clusters of single-room houses, built of the local flagstone even to their internal furnishings, were founded by stone-using communities who kept domesticated flocks and herds and grew cereal crops. The earliest settlers must have come by boat from the Scottish mainland to the islands, bringing with them enough sheep, cattle and goats to breed new flocks and herds. That they did not attempt pig-breeding is perhaps another indication of the lack of woodland, for the pig is a forest beast, rooting for acorns and similar food. From the possessions of the Skara Brae and Rinyo folk, we can trace their affinities with other Neolithic groups in Britain. They made distinctive pottery of types known as far south as the English

Channel coast, and worked extensively in bone (including whale bone), and sometimes in walrus ivory, making pins (probably to skewer a greasy bun of hair into place). The decorative patterns with which they ornamented their pottery or scratched on the stones of their huts again repeat Irish motifs of the time. All this points to contacts with the western seaways, along which in this period was a brisk trafficking, and in general to connections with the world of western Europe.

The famous stone-built houses of Skara Brae (199), built and occupied between about 3000 to 2400 BC, may be an adaptation to northern traditions. Dug into the sand and linked each to each in the settlement by narrow roofed passages or alleyways, they are of uniform plan, a square with rounded corners, about 4.5 m across, with a single narrow door and a central square hearth on which peat was burned. Built against the walls on each side of the door are slab-constructed bed frames, doubtless once filled with heather, and upright stone posts to take a protective skin cover that would minimise the discomforts of a leaky roof. Opposite the door, against the wall on the other side of the hearth, are stone-built shelves constituting nothing more nor less than a dresser, facing the visitor exactly as its wooden counterpart does in many a cottage today. Little square slab-lined boxes let into the floors probably held water and a supply of fresh shell-fish. Keeping-places or small cupboards are contrived in the thick dry-stone walls. Lack of suitable timber led to the use of flagstone where wood would have been more appropriate, and so preserved for posterity this domestic detail for nearly five thousand years.

These semi-subterranean houses were roofed probably by sods over a low conical structure of driftwood or even whales' bones, and in the later stages of the settlement were covered by layers of accumulated midden soil and drifted sand: when you live half underground the best place for the rubbish dump is on top. Beneath it, in semi-darkness and squalor, where the light would come from the peat fire or at best blubber lamps, and where the floor was slippery with stinking filth and a calf's head could get lost among the bedding, the Neolithic inhabi-

Skara Brae: linking passage

33

tants of Orkney could at least be warm and out of the wind that howled across Skaill Bay and down Eynhallow Sound.

In Shetland at about this time settlements of people who grew barley and lived in substantial stone-built houses had been established. Here there was no dense aggregation of inter-communicating huts, but the individual houses were scattered among the pastures and arable fields exactly like modern crofts. The houses, with dry-built walls sometimes with a core of peats or ash, were oval in shape with an entrance at one end, which was flattened to form a sort of façade. Around the houses the remains of ancient field walls show the enclosures for stock and arable.

One building, at Stanydale (164), of similar plan but of more elaborate construction and of much greater size (12 m by 6.7 m internally) has been called a temple. Its plan is indeed related to those of the monumental collective chambered tombs, which might suggest a religious purpose, and which were built by these people in common with many other related com-munities in west and north Scotland at this time. But it is when we come to interpretations such as this that purely archaeological evidence begins to show its weaknesses. The building at Stanydale could have been used as a temple, but equally as a chieftain's house if the social structure of the Shetland communities included a ruling class. Or it could have been a communal building or 'club house' of the kind used for instance in Borneo and the Pacific islands today. We must confess ignorance: houses of the living and houses of the dead may share similar ground plans without relation of purpose. An interesting point in the construction of the Stanydale building is that the roofing must have involved a considerable quantity of timber – some 750 linear metres in fact – and one of the massive uprights holding the ridge-pole was of spruce, a tree which is not indigenous in Britain, and which must have been available in Shetland as drift-timber from North Ameri-ca. We have a much later example of its use in the Hebrides in the early centuries AD, again clearly from the same source.

So far we have been considering settlements and houses, but the most striking monuments in Scotland of the third millennium B C are the stone-built chambered tombs of the collective burial of several persons – the family vaults of forgotten dynasties and nameless communities. Burial customs varied, and not every group in Neolithic Scotland buried in chambered tombs: on Cairnpapple Hill (129) in West Lothian, for instance, a little cemetery of cremated burials put into holes in the ground has been found, and with the burnt bones were bits of bone or ivory pins like those from Skara Brae. But along the western sea-ways of the British Isles communities with a long tradition of building monumental burial places for their dead were established, and though the actual settlements of these people are hardly known, their chambered tombs survive to show us the areas which they colonised.

The collective tomb built above ground developed especially in the West, and in particular the technique of the so-called false vault, in which a chamber is roofed by successive oversailing courses of stone, or corbels, was evolved. To make such a vault secure and permanent, and to enhance the monumental quality of the building, a covering of stones – a cairn – bounded by a retaining wall at its foot, was also developed, through which the burial chamber was approached by a roofed passage so that successive burials could be brought in to their final resting-place. Two basic types seem to have been devised quite early on, either circular or oblong in the plan of both chamber and covering mound. As alternatives to roofing with the false vault, where suitable slabby stone did not occur, the simpler but more massive construction of large flat slabs supported on uprights was used.

It must be remembered that the construction of these tombs, with their various modifications such as multiple chambers, elaborated entrances and forecourts, and other variants on the basic plan, was dictated by the funeral ceremonies for which they were the architectural setting. In their study, it is instructive to bear in mind the variants on the theme of the early Christian and mediaeval church plan: the differences in lay-out that divergent rituals dictated, as between the eastern and the western churches, the elongation of the chancels of collegiate establishments, the provision of chantry chapels and shrines, as well as the post-Reformation development of

35

the 'auditory church' with its liturgical centre shifted from altar to pulpit. In the chambered tombs, as in the Christian churches (or Islamic mosques), we seem to see the products of a common cult expressed in characteristic religious architecture. But we do not know, nor can archaeology tell us, the beliefs and rituals enshrined in these structures.

It is difficult to determine how much the appearance of this new cult, with its appropriate ritual structures, owed to actual colonisation by people bringing with them not only their religious traditions but their seed-corn and their individual styles in household equipment, and how much it was due to local invention and development. Both may have occurred. Objects of local styles and traditions buried with the dead seem to imply that little beyond the cult and the architectural techniques connected with it can be detected. But the close correspondence between the architectural modes of many of the chambered tombs suggests that we have remarkable evidence for the sea voyages at the time. Even when one allows for coasting movements wherever possible, this does not minimise the hazards of exploring the western approaches to the Outer Isles, Orkney and Shetland.

In south-west Scotland, in Galloway, in the islands round the Clyde estuary, and up into the Hebrides, long-chambered tombs are found beneath even more elongated mounds (up to 45 m long), often with the entrance demarcated by an elaborate semi-circular forecourt marked by tall upright stones. The plan of these tombs is in some respects similar to that of those of the Severn estuary and the Cotswold region of England, and to a greater degree to tombs in Ulster, which may represent a parallel implantation of tradition on the other side of the Irish Sea, or perhaps colonisation from Scotland. Except for their forecourts, these tombs do not embody any notable architecture. The rather scanty objects buried with the dead, including food-offerings, show us that we are dealing with agriculturalists breeding cattle and sheep, and their situation on patches of good alluvial soil near coasts or estuaries suggests the choice of suitable farming land. From one of these tombs, at Cairnholy

Cairnholy chambered tomb: façade

(48) near Creetown in Galloway, came a piece of one of the ceremonial jadeite axe-blades mentioned earlier, and which was evidently treasured even as a fragment.

In Ireland the tomb with false-vaulted chamber beneath a circular mound had developed to a remarkable degree of individual elaboration, and it is probably with Ireland rather than the Continent that the Scottish tombs of this type may have their likely affinities. The simpler form, the basic theme on which both Ireland and Scotland executed remarkable variations, is known however in both countries. In Scotland, in Glen Urquhart, by the Beauly Firth, around Inverness and Nairn, and even in the valley of the Spey near Aviemore, are chambered tombs of a considerable degree of architectural competence, although their false-vaulted circular chambers are not of great size (about 3.6 m in diameter). Here too are tombs with an unroofed circular area in their centre in which cremated burials were placed (as in the Clava group (99) near Culloden). No metal objects have been found in any of the chambered tombs in the British Isles, and in Ireland their building goes back to the fifth millennium BC.

The most impressive chambered tombs in Scotland are, however, those in Caithness and Orkney whose architecture represents local developments. The tombs of the Caithness region, and southwards to the Black Isle, seem to show a mixture of traditions derived from both long and round types. The Grey Cairns of Camster (93) in Caithness, one round, one hugely elongated, are among the finest examples, and in the round cairn is a great false-vaulted burial chamber with the roof rising to some 4 m above the floor. But it is on the Mainland island of Orkney that the finest chambered tomb in Britain was built – that known as Maes Howe (143). The chamber and approach passage are covered by a great mound of earth 7.3 m high and 35 m in diameter, with a revetted stone core, which stands within a nearly circular shallow ditch enclosing an area 76 m by 60 m across. The passage, 11 m long, is, like the rest of the structure, built of enormous slabs of the local flagstone up to 5.6 m long, so that much of its length is composed of three stones only. The entrance was provided with a huge stone block which could be used to close it, or be

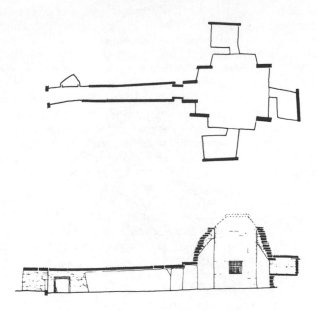

Maes Howe: plan and elevation

levered back into a recess in the wall contrived to hold it. The chamber is an astonishing tour-de-force of construction. It is a square of 4.6 m in plan, each corner containing an attached pier which runs up to support an angle of the corbelled or false-vaulted roof in the manner of squinches supporting a dome. In constructing the roof, of huge slabs in oversailing courses, the builders utilised the fact that the flagstone splits naturally to form an edge at a slight angle to its flat sides, and arranged the slabs so that the slightly diagonal edges meet one against another to carry on an almost smooth slope for as much of the vault as is constructionally possible. This remarkable refinement of technique is matched by the stone-work of the walls, so jointed that a penknife blade can scarcely be inserted between the huge blocks. From the three walls of the chamber not occupied by the passage entrance, small compartments open above ground level. These probably originally contained

39

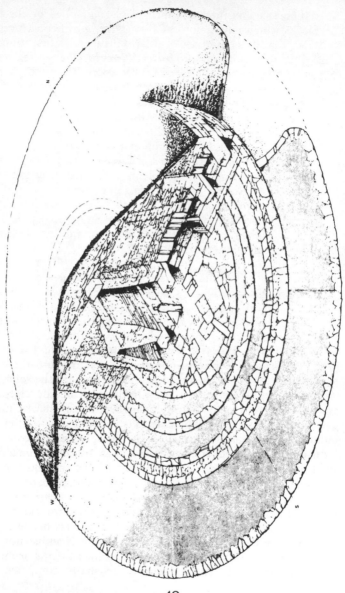

the burials, and their entrances were once filled by the big blocks which now lie on the floor. The date of construction was probably around 2700 BC. Unfortunately this princely sepulchre was broken into by the Vikings in the twelfth century, who recorded the fact in inscriptions scratched on the chamber walls, and who despoiled the tomb of whatever it may have contained.

The consummate craftsmanship of Maes Howe, with its implications of a carefully thought-out design – one might almost say, of an individual architect – and of the command of labour necessary to put such a grandiose scheme into execution, raises in acute form problems as fascinating as they are difficult of solution, which are also presented by the other great chambered tombs or, in an even more outstanding manner, by the building of the final phase of Stonehenge. What, in short, was the social structure of the communities who built these monuments? A settlement like Skara Brae suggests no disparity in wealth or status between the inhabitants of the various huts, and it has been suggested that the building of the smaller chambered tombs, such as those on Rousay or again those of south-west Scotland, involved no more labour or skill than that which was at the disposal of small crofting settlements who wished to provide themselves with a family or clan burying-place. But at Camster or Maes Howe, and at other Orkney tombs like Quanterness (145), Quoyness (146) or Wideford Hill (154), and again in Ireland where the great chambered tombs form cemeteries by the Boyne or on the Meath and Sligo hilltops, we have surely the reflection of a society more stratified than the squalid egalitarianism of Skara Brae. However constituted, the social system under which such monuments could be built must have involved some command of labour and technical skill concentrated in an individual – chieftain, priest or priest-chieftain – or in a ruling caste.

The communities who built the northern Scottish chambered tombs seem on the whole to have shared the local traditions of handicrafts. Contacts with Ireland may however, be implied in the use of certain magical symbols, especially the

Quanterness in 3000 BC: a reconstruction

stylised face represented by a pair of eyes which may be drawn as spirals. The magic eyes look out from a stone in the chambered tomb on the Holm of Papa Westray (138); as spirals they are carved on a stone from Rousay, incised on pottery from Skara Brae, and on one of the curious carved stone balls of this period from north-east Scotland.

Among Neolithic communities in the British Isles we see, in more than one region, the construction of what must have been open circular sanctuaries enclosed or delimited by a bank and ditch with a single entrance. In some of these, there is no evidence of anything standing within the enclosing *temenos* – examples are known in Scotland – but some had standing stones and timber rings, as at Balfarg (59) in Fife, and the Stones of Stenness (151) in Orkney (with a date around 2900 B C).

A variant on the type has two entrances, one opposite the other, and frequently a ring of standing stones within the enclosed area. It includes some of the best-known Scottish antiquities, notably the Ring of Brodgar (148) in Orkney – the great circles of Avebury in Wiltshire form part of an aberrant monument of the same general series. In West Lothian on Cairnpapple Hill, excavation showed that the standing stones of a sanctuary site of this kind had been dismantled, and almost certainly then used on their sides as the retaining kerb of a burial cairn on the same site, but of a slightly later phase, with a food-vessel pot with the central interment. Here, in fact, we have a curious glimpse of some change in outlook which allowed a not-so-ancient sanctuary to be demolished and to be replaced by a monumental cairn-burial. Simple or complex stone circles and individual standing stones are widespread in Scotland, and while each example is usually difficult to date, they must on the whole fall within the third and second millennia B C. At Croft Moraig (228) in Perthshire the stone settings were preceded by timber uprights.

Somewhere in this same position of time and circumstance we must also place these enigmatic carvings on natural rock surfaces, or less often on the stones of burial cists, which

Maes Howe: interior of chamber

consist of 'cups and rings' – central cups surrounded by concentric and usually penannular rings (see Index of Sites). In one
respect these should be related to the somewhat similar stone
carvings of the makers of chambered tombs in Ireland and less
frequently in Wales and Britain, and in another with very
comparable carvings on natural rocks in the north of Spain.
There is some reason to think that the cup-and-ring patterns,
evidently endowed with symbolic significance to their car-
vers, may be derived from a simple maze or labyrinth design
widespread throughout the ancient and modern world. We
shall find them, together with other related patterns, still
being carved in North Britain at a time when bronze-working
had been established, and when technologically the British
Isles had entered the Bronze Age.

The events connected with this ancient industrial revolution are the subject-matter of the next section. We shall see
how Scotland, together with the rest of Britain, seems to enter
into a phase of dual relationships, brought about by continental contacts with the east coasts and by the development of
connections with the west, especially with Ireland, with her
natural resources of copper and gold, and with Cornwall, rich
in tin.

Ring of Brodgar, Orkney, showing the stone-cut ditch

III

Throughout the history of technology – and this after all forms the content of so much of archaeology – we are dealing with the invention, dispersal and exchange of ideas and techniques between communities. An innovation in craftsmanship, in the production and working of raw materials, or in the means and manner of subsistence, has first to be devised by an individual and then to be accepted by the members of the group to which he belongs. If an invention is not socially acceptable to family, clan or tribe, it may never, in simple or primitive communities, go further than a bright idea in a mind less bound by traditions of conservatism than those of the rest of the group. In modern industrialised societies the idea of technological development (often known as progress) rates high in the group's esteem, but we should make a grave mistake if we regarded this attitude as one universal to mankind.

It is therefore of great importance to remember such facts when we come to consider what appear to be revolutionary technological changes in prehistory. In the nineteenth century, when an increasing complexity of technology and material culture was confidently equated by many with a corresponding move of man towards the angels, the concept of ancient man moving inevitably, and indeed eagerly, from a Stone to a Bronze, from a Bronze to an Iron Age, in a God-guided progress all over the world, was acceptable enough. But as the study of prehistory and anthropology developed, the process was seen to be anything but a simple and orderly one. We had, it became apparent, to deal with areas or communities with a tradition of innovation in the technical fields, and over against these were other traditions of conservatism and, so far as the development of material equipment went, stagnation. Communities which had succeeded in evolving economies elaborately adjusted to, and closely interwoven with, a natural habitat in which conditions might be hard and unfavourable would not disturb a precariously balanced but ingeniously devised rhythm of life which at least sufficed for a reasonable existence in those particular circumstances.

We have already seen that the beginnings of agriculture and stock-breeding in prehistoric Scotland, as elsewhere in the British Isles, was the result of the actual immigration of groups of people, themselves already skilled in the techniques of the farmer. They came ultimately from the European continent, and their own agricultural ancestry stretched back to western Asia, the greatest and most formative area of innovation in the Old World. But by the time Britain was being populated by the first stone-using farmers, the Ancient Orient had reached a stage of mastery over metal-working equal to that of mediaeval Europe.

The change-over from a stone-using to a metal-using economy involves more than the substitution of a better substance for tools, weapons and ornaments. Compared with workable stones, the natural ores and deposits of metal are rare and widely distributed. To obtain the raw material involves prospecting journeys, or interchange of commodities, or both, and increased contact with other communities, perhaps over long distances. A man ceases to be self-sufficient, and may place his group in a position of obligation or treaty relationship with others seeking or controlling the metal sources, or occupying territory on routes of access. Again, the techniques

47

of the metal-smith are in themselves complex, and entail more than a rudimentary knowledge of surface geology, as well as the practical chemistry involved in smelting, alloying, casting and the related processes. Such secrets of the craft are difficult to acquire, and not to be cheapened by indiscriminate dissemination to all and sundry: they give prestige to the individual and to his tribe, and must be jealously guarded.

It is not surprising then that the techniques of early metallurgy, involving the use of copper, bronze (the copper-tin alloy) and gold, spread slowly and often sporadically and incompletely through prehistoric Europe. The British Isles are among those regions of western Europe where copper and gold occur in natural deposits. More important still, that much rarer metal tin, essential for bronze, is found in Cornwall. It was as a result of these metal resources that the British Isles became at an early stage one of the formative areas of technological development in Bronze Age Europe.

When we are assessing the metal resources available to prehistoric man in Britain, we must remember that, in at least the earlier stages of metallurgy, surface deposits or outcrops alone were exploited, and mining was carried out only at a later date, and then in restricted areas of Europe. Scotland offers good metal resources which can be won by simple methods, and takes its place with Ireland and north-west England as one of the main areas where copper and gold can be obtained in the British Isles. Copper could, and almost certainly was, obtained from such localities as the Leadhills and the Ochils, around Crinan and Loch Fyne, by Loch Ness and the North Esk, and from other less rewarding deposits which occur sporadically from the Lammermuirs to Wick. Gold also could be obtained in the Leadhills district, in the region of Loch Tay and Loch Earn, and in Strath Brora and Helmsdale. But Scotland, like the rest of the British Isles, was throughout the period of bronze-using dependent on Cornwall (or the Continent) for its tin supplies, so that a necessary connection between the north and the south-west of Britain, by whatever indirect routes and between however many middlemen, was necessarily established at an early date in the second millennium B C.

Although no objects of metal have been recorded from the

primary burials in the collective tombs of the types described in the last chapter, we must always remember, when dealing with what one may call 'grave archaeology' (with which we must now largely deal), that the ritual prescription of what shall or shall not be buried with the dead may bear little relationship to the relative richness or poverty of the material culture of the people involved. Indeed, we see later in this chapter how, with the general adoption of cremation-burial in Britain, before the middle of the second millennium BC, the practice of placing objects with the dead (especially weapons with the men) was almost entirely given up, although we know that a rich equipment in bronze tools and weapons was in fact available.

In the early second millennium BC, a force in the development of early metal-working in the British Isles was provided from northern Europe. Known by their very individual types of drinking vessels, or beakers, a new element or cultural tradition in the population shows connections with a fairly restricted region of the North European plain between the Oder and the Meuse. The movements involved are complex, but one can trace regional relationships between Britain and specific areas of the Continent, such as the Netherlands and the lower Rhine.

In addition to the appearance of a novel type of pottery, an alternative burial rite to that normal in the chambered tombs now appears: that of individual, not collective, burial, in which the dead person is placed in a single grave, which in some of the communities involved was normally covered by a more or less monumental cairn or barrow. One might see in this (but probably dangerous anachronistically) the underlying concept of a more individualistic view of the dead man's journey to the Otherworld than that implicit in the huddled anonymity of the burials in a chambered tomb. This too might be thought to be emphasised by the frequent practice of burying with the dead personal possessions appropriate to their sex and status – elaborate necklaces with women, or the bronze knife-dagger and archery equipment with men – in a manner unlike the meagre and impersonal offerings which at best accompany the collective burials in Britain.

49

There is little evidence that the early communities of beaker-makers utilised metal to any great extent, though we should remember the warning about the potentially misleading character of the grave-archaeology with which we are dealing. However, several copper daggers from Scotland are of types used by such communities in central Europe and the Netherlands, and some of the many finds of flat, copper or bronze, axe-blades (very rarely placed in graves anywhere) may also have been made or imported by them. We shall note that in fact the main centres of early metalworking in Scotland (as shown by finds of moulds for casting such axe-blades) are not those likely to have been populated by the beaker-making communities we are considering here. Like their Continental ancestors, they were archers, and on occasion buried with the dead man his flint-tipped arrows and archer's bracer or wrist-guard, made of a little plaque of finely worked stone which would be strapped on the inside of the left wrist to take the 'kick' of the recoiling bow-string. The bow, wholly of perishable materials, has not survived, and, if it were the long 'self' bow in one piece, could, unless ritually broken, hardly have been contained in the smallish grave or cist which holds the normal crouched-up burial : the shorter 'composite' bow incorporating horn and sinew might be accommodated, but there is no direct evidence of its use by these peoples.

These people were agriculturalists, who appear to have grown barley as their main crop; cereal grains accidentally incorporated in the surface of the soft clay of an unbaked pot have burnt out on firing, leaving an accurate identifiable cast. This elegant technique of identification has materially increased our knowledge of prehistoric agriculture in many periods. We know little of the settlements, although some certainly existed among the sand dunes in such regions as Glenluce in Galloway, Gullane and North Berwick in East Lothian, Tentsmuir in Fife and Ardnamurchan in Argyll; extensive remains of plough cultivation, indicating the use of the simple type of plough known as a crook ard, used in the initial breaking-up of new land, have been found in the dunes at

Grave group, Culduthel, Inverness (above); crouched burial

Rosinish on Benbecula.

The Scottish burials of this period were normally in stone-slabbed cists or ordinary graves, in which the dead person was buried in a crouched position, knees to chin, on occasion with a pottery vessel of one of the so-called beaker types, which may well have contained drink. But a number of otherwise similar graves have a pottery vessel of a distinct form, a biconical or bowl-shaped food-vessel (as the type is called, perhaps with good reason), with no Continental parallels and many features which suggest native Neolithic traditions of pottery form and ornament. It may be significant that practically no grave with such a pot contains anything (such as a battle-axe or dagger) to suggest a specifically male burial, but that a number of them do contain either small flint knives or elaborate jet necklaces more appropriate to women. These necklaces have a great interest when one comes to consider their origins and relationships, as we shall see.

We know something of the costume of these people, at least by inference. In the first place, while woollen cloth may well have been woven at this time, as it was slightly later, there is every likelihood that leather garments continued to be worn, particularly in regions where the climate demanded their warmth and comfort. Fur coats and leather jerkins are not to be despised at any time in Scotland! When we came to look at the question of the basic types of clothing possible to early men in Europe – and in Eurasia – we saw two traditions represented in the archaeological and early historical material available. On the one hand there are the simple untailored garments of the type of the burnous or toga, which are simply lengths of cloth wound round the body in varying ways, and involving little beyond a capacity for weaving fabric to an adequate breadth. This is basically the garment of the Ancient East and the Classical World of the Mediterranean. But in northern Europe and Asia (and for that matter among the Eskimos and the North American Indians) the use of skins for clothing in cold and damp conditions produced a garment cut to shape and

Reconstruction of Bronze Age hut, Machrie, Arran (above);
Ardmarks near Thurso, Caithness (below)

sewn together so as to make an artificial skin or fur covering for a hairless man, as near as possible to the natural prototype among the animals. In other words, trousers and sleeved jackets are developed, and once the horse is domesticated, trousers take on an added importance as a garment well suited for riding. It could be then that the tailored garment, which in one form or another most of us Europeans wear today, is an invention of Mesolithic, if not Upper Palaeolithic times.

Prehistoric clothing is rarely preserved in Europe, but its fastenings are often more durable. Pins and brooches fasten cloaks and togas, while buttons are more appropriate for jerkins of skin or tailored cloth. An archaeological survey of the distribution of pins and buttons in early second millennium Europe is, therefore, not just a piece of meaningless typology, but a survey of broad trends in the fashion of dress. And when we make such a survey, we see the British Isles falling within a north-western province in which buttoned garments were the vogue, while central Europe, for instance, favoured clothing fastened by pins of varied forms. Among the beaker- and food-vessel-using people in Britain, large conical jet or shale buttons were popular, and a Scottish find (from Angus), where five buttons were found spaced out in a row 100 mm apart, shows how they must have been sewn on the vanished garment, which would have measured the very reasonable length of 400 mm from neck to waist. Whether trousers were worn at this time in Britain we do not know, for their first demonstrable appearance in our prehistory is with the appearance of the Celts in the last centuries B C. The early history and prehistory of the kilt and plaid in its original unitary form is unknown: it would have been, as we have seen, a member of the simple toga class of garment, though appearing in an area where not only would one expect the dominance of the tailored clothes tradition, but one in which the trousered Celt had played a decisive part. The alternatives would seem either to regard the traditional undivided kilt and plaid as the product of a late degeneration in the technological standards of clothes production, or conceivably (if we knew that its history stretched so far back) as a native copy of a Roman fashion.

General considerations suggest that the techniques of early

Scottish metal-working are likely to have had technical affinities with those of Ireland, though some contact with the European continent is not impossible. Whatever may have been the mechanics of the process, we have seen that local sources for copper ore were available, though once technology advanced from a copper-working to a bronze-working economy, the necessity for tin as an alloy must have meant relationships with Cornwall. The types of copper and bronze tools and weapons produced in Scotland in the early second millennium B C, or acquired by trade, basically represent the traditions of the metal-smiths of European workshops. Flat knives or daggers, fastened by rivets to their hafts of wood, bone or horn, and flat axe-blades with wooden shafts, were among the most important products of the local smiths, though metal was sufficiently abundant in Scotland for massive solid bronze bracelets to be cast, of a simple but distinctive type unknown

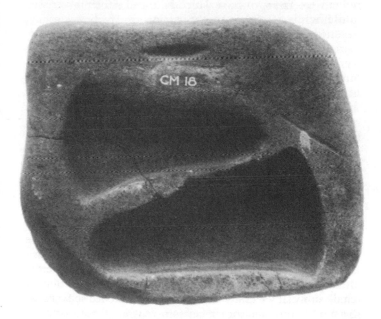

Mould for flat axes and awl

elsewhere in the British Isles. It is unlikely that pure ornaments using a great deal of bronze would be made until the
need for edge tools had first been satisfied. Technically, the
casting processes were of the simplest, involving little beyond
an open flat mould of stone into which the molten metal could
be poured. More complicated valve-mould and other casting
processes were not mastered until many years later in Britain.

At this point we must, for the time being, leave the Scottish
scene with its little communities growing grain in roughly
hoed or ard-cultivated patches, breeding cattle, goats and
sheep, making attractive pottery and ornaments, and working
and trading in copper, gold and bronze. Similar communities
were now, around 1500 BC, established over the greater part of
northern and western Europe, but in the Aegean, the Minoan
civilisation was already old. On the Greek mainland those
whom we know to have been the Greeks themselves were
building up a composite civilisation in which the ancient
traditions of Crete and the Near East were blended with a more
barbarian strain of heroes and horsemen, panache and chariotry, to make the world of the palaces of Mycenae and Pylos,
distortingly and dimly remembered in the *Iliad* and the *Odyssey*. It was technologically a Bronze Age world, with metal in
high demand for the equipment of the prince and his palace, a
world of trading and voyaging that is reflected not only in
Homer but in the exploits of the Argonauts. Necklaces of
amber from the shores of the North Sea in the princely tombs
of Mycenaean Greece are amusing instances of vanity calling
for the exotic alike in Greece and Britain, but there is little
doubt that it was the metal trade, and especially that in Corn-
ish tin, which was the mainspring of contact in north-west
Europe.

As a result of this intensified interchange network involved
in the use of, and search for, metals, from areas stimulated by it
such as central Europe, the British Isles were brought into a
position of some considerable European importance. On the
chalk downs of Wessex, lying on a natural route between the
Bristol Channel and the western sea-ways on the one hand, and
the coasts of the English Channel and the North Sea on the

other, metal-working techniques were improved, largely by contact with central European workshops, and there grew up what has been called the Wessex Culture of the British Bronze Age, notable for its wealth and originality, and roughly spanning the centuries 1600–1350 BC.

The Wessex chieftains began by burying their dead under barrows in the traditional manner of their ancestors, but later adopted the practice of cremation. In Scotland (as in Ireland and much of northern England) the inhumation rite was similarly replaced by that of cremation. In the north of Britain we find that instead of burial beneath a barrow, it is more usual to bury the ashes of the dead man in a family burying-place. Such cremation cemeteries may contain up to twenty or so burials, all by cremation and usually with the burnt bones enclosed in a pottery vessel or cinerary urn. Some have no surface indication today (though when in use, the graves must have been marked in some way to avoid disturbance by subsequent burials), but some are enclosed by circles of standing stones, or banks and ditches which carry on the tradition of the Neolithic circular ditched sanctuaries. The main pottery container for the ashes may be accompanied, as elsewhere in Britain, by a small finely made cup, which is so distinctive and recurrent in such graves as to suggest that it had some ritual function at the funeral.

We can only guess at the rituals that must have accompanied these burials. The body would have been cremated on a funeral pyre, and we can often see that the burnt bones have been carefully separated from the wood ashes before they were placed in the urn. These urns were almost certainly not made for burial purposes alone, but were household storage jars used for funerary ends. Frequently they are buried inverted, evidently covered by cloth or leather tied down over the moulded rim of the pot, to prevent the bones from falling out! Such covers would have been equally useful for the mundane purpose of preserving the contents of a storage vessel.

Many of these burials have nothing except the pottery vessels with them, many more have only the single containing urn, and some cremations are even deposited directly in the earth in a container of some now-perished substance such as

'Urn found near Banff', from Pennant 1769

skin or cloth. But some have objects with them which show that Scotland was taking a part in the general pattern of trade at the time, namely pins of central European types, bronze daggers with gold hilts similar to those of Wessex. In Orkney a cremation burial under one of the barrows known as The Knowes of Trotty (141) had not only decorative gold discs with it, but re-used fragments of an amber necklace of a type known in Britain in the Wessex graves, and also found in central Europe.

The Knowes of Trotty necklace, almost certainly an import from Wessex, is interesting in connection with a large number of similarly constructed 'chokers' known from graves in Scotland and northern England, but made in the locally available lignite or jet. It is fairly certain that these jet necklaces must be the counterparts, in another relatively precious substance, of those of amber found in Wiltshire. The same is true of the more spectacular sheet-gold crescents, or lunulae, known from Scotland but more frequent in Ireland, the ornament of which follows the arrangement of beads and spacing-beads on the necklaces.

We have no more than hints of the possible social structure of these second-millennium communities in Scotland, or indeed elsewhere in Britain. The graves of the Wessex chieftains just described can be taken to imply some sort of society in which a warrior aristocracy played a part. Such a social system, with a graded series of obligations of service from a king or princeling, through a military nobility, down to the craftsmen and peasants, was common in the ancient world. We have no knowledge of the languages spoken in Britain before the advent of the Celtic-speaking peoples, but some have thought it not impossible that dialects with origins within the Indo-European language group might have been in existence at an early date.

It is important at this point to remember that whereas today the Celtic languages are spoken, or were recently spoken, on the extreme north-western fringe of Europe, from Brittany through Wales and Ireland to Scotland, the homeland of the Celtic-speaking peoples lay in central Europe east of the Rhine. The distribution-pattern of the languages today represents the result of centuries of movement and migration westwards and northwards, and their survival is due to their peripheral position, where they have survived unsubmerged by the later tides of Romance and Teutonic dialects. Linguistically, the separation of the variant which was to become the Celtic languages from the common Indo-European stock, could have been an early event, so that we have a reasonable case for assuming that by 1000 BC at least, the peoples in central Europe, who are later known to have been speaking Celtic dialects, were already, in the linguistic sense, Celts. This is the only sense in which the word can be used – Celts are people who speak Celtic, whatever mixed racial characteristics they may embody.

To return to Scotland and the British Isles (though we will see that our Celtic expedition has not been without point), the centuries following the middle second millennium BC are, in

the north and west, a rather obscure phase of comparative isolation from Continental movements. The metal industry, now well established and flourishing, was embarking on various technical innovations, in common with that of the Continent. Bronze casting in closed valve-moulds of two or more pieces was now a commonplace, with the result that more complex and elaborate forms of axes, spears, daggers and rapiers were made possible. Such contacts as we can perceive at this time in Scotland (about 1300–700 BC) seem to have been mainly with Ireland, and the Continental relationships which, probably from about 1000 BC onwards, affected southern England did not touch the north. When we do see Continental connections revived in the seventh century BC, they seem to link Scotland and northern England with regions and traditions different from those affecting the south.

It is difficult to assess the relative contributions to the last phase of bronze-using technologies in Europe of outside influences, and indigenous traditions developing on their own. But certain technical innovations, notably the use of beaten bronze metal-work for such things as cups or cauldrons or helmets, which now become known in central Europe, could be of Oriental origin, perhaps brought by displaced craftsmen seeking employment among European barbarians. Other innovations were brought about by modifications in fighting techniques such as the adoption of the slashing sword in place of the dagger or rapier, and the use of the horse as a traction animal.

North of the Alps, over a broad belt of territory stretching from Burgundy to Bohemia, which by this time was almost certainly Celtic, we can see, from about 800 BC onwards, evidence of a warrior-aristocracy much concerned with driving, and probably riding, horses, and decking their steeds with elaborate trappings of leather and bronze. This interest in horses (going back to earlier traditions of chariotry in eastern Europe as well as in the ancient Oriental world, and also comparable with that of the Scythians and similar peoples of the steppes) remained a feature of the Celtic world until his-

Aberlemno, Angus: jet necklace

torical times. In the British Isles we can date its earliest appearance to these final phases of the bronze-using technologies which we are discussing. It may be that with it we should connect the arrival of some at least of our Celtic-speaking ancestors.

Britain, as so often in prehistory and early history, was at this time – from the eighth or ninth century BC – very much the converging point of two lines of trade, one from central Europe and one along the western sea-ways. In Scotland, from the seventh century onwards, we can see the reflection of the major movements we have been indicating in the form of bronzes of novel types, soon to be manufactured in the north. Great globular bronze cauldrons, up to o.6 m across, represent the western European version of the Greek *dinos*; similarly fashioned buckets reflect central European schools of metal-work. Such vessels are of Irish or North British manufacture, but occasionally actual foreign imports can be identified, like the fragments of a seventh-century central European bowl from Adabrock in Lewis. In Peeblesshire a bronze-smith hid among the screes on a hillside a stock of scrap metal which was largely made up of harness and cart fittings; elsewhere fork-like objects, likely to be horse-goads, have been found, and so in Scotland as in the rest of the British Isles we have the first intimation of horsemanship.

The technique of complicated bronze-casting was now common, especially for making the socketed axe-blades which all over Europe had replaced the less securely hafted earlier forms, and the heavy slashing leaf-shaped swords which had come into fashion. There must have been much coming and going, perhaps as often piratical as peaceful, on the sea-ways around the Scottish coasts and the routes between Scandinavia and Ireland. It is surely only in some sort of setting of sea-raiding that we can explain how a bronze-smith was able at this time to set up shop on Sumburgh Head in Shetland, and produce not only axe-blades but the long swords as well. The debris of his foundry, with its litter of broken clay moulds, shows he was actively engaged in such manufacture, and who but warlike

Bivalve spear moulds

seafarers needing swords would be likely to trade with such a remote workshop?

From at least the ninth century BC southern England had been in touch with communities across the Channel. A developed form of agriculture, based on the traction plough and a regular field-system, together with pasturage or ranch areas delimited by permanent land divisions, had long been established on the Continent and in Britain. Upon this basis there grew up a cereal-growing economy which was ultimately to become the granary of the Roman province in Britain. As far as Scotland and northern England are concerned (and probably Ireland as well), intensive corn-growing of this kind has not been recognised as yet, and a more varied agricultural pattern may have existed. We may, in some regions at least, have to reckon with restricted subsistence cultivation at best, or to envisage forms of shifting agriculture and perhaps some in the manner of early historic Ireland. There has been considerable debate as to whether in the world of Celtic Britain as we shall see it in the centuries immediately before, and during, the Roman Occupation, there were these two strains of agricultural economy, and evidence for pastoralism is inevitably elusive.

Hard on the heels of the final stages of bronze technology in north-west Europe follows the knowledge of the use of iron, and we move into a world of iron-using communities in Britain from at least the seventh century BC onwards. But there is essential continuity from earlier centuries, and though it may have been a period of movement and unrest, yet, with the phase preceding it which we have just surveyed, it is one dominated by Celtic-speaking peoples.

IV

From the seventh century BC several communities in Britain seem to have been acquainted with iron-working, from York-shire to Dorset. The subsistence-pattern of these people, who archaeologically usher in the Early Iron Age and must have spoken some form of Celtic language, seems to have been based on the single steading or isolated farmhouse rather than the nucleated village; the old field-systems of the chalk lands were increased in area, and a prosperous population engaged in mixed farming, growing cereal crops and with flocks and herds of cattle, sheep, goats and pigs, was spread over large areas of Wessex, Sussex, the Thames Valley and beyond. But a new feature appears, all too significant in a Celtic context – an increase in hill-top fortifications designed to protect people and stock from inter-tribal warfare and cattle-reiving. Such hill-forts begin the story of military architecture in Britain, and have indigenous origins which may go back to the second millennium BC.

The descendants of these people were to be encountered by Caesar in his campaigns, and we can regard their language with some certainty as a version of the earlier 'Common Celtic' known as Gallo-Brittonic. They adopted a new offensive weapon, the horse-drawn war chariot, which was to continue in employment in Britain for some centuries after it was outmoded on the Continent. Before the first century BC further immigrations or refugee movements seem to have contributed to the British Celtic population, notably the members of Belgic tribes, who before 100 BC made an entry into south-east England.

The decisive Celticisation of Britain then (excluding Ireland, which constitutes a special problem) was the result of complex European contacts. In the south, and especially on the Wessex and Sussex chalk downs, an elaborate and productive corn-growing economy was developed on the basis of earlier agricultural techniques and agrarian systems, but in more northerly regions cereal production seems to have been less intensive.

The first few centuries BC were, like those which were to follow the fall of the Roman Empire, a time of movement and migration of peoples; of displaced persons and refugees; of fugitives from the threat of Roman rule or from internecine wars among their own people. The Celts, originating in the second millennium BC in central Europe east of the Rhine, had greatly enlarged their territory by raids and migrations. They had penetrated to the Iberian peninsula, sacked Rome in 386 BC, within a century raided Delphi, and established a colony (Galatia) in Asia Minor. From Galatia to Britain is some 3,000 km in a straight line, and in 250 BC an imaginary aircraft following this route could have flown over Celtic-speaking peoples from end to end of its course. But remarkable though the range of Celtic expansion was, it was never an empire, nor was it ever more than a scattering of clans and tribes sharing common languages, common social organisation and religious traditions. Entering into temporary alliances, but constantly disrupted by internal warfare and by instability of purpose and action, the sphere of loyalty of the Celt was as limited, and as easily transferred, as that of the other barbarian tribes of northern Europe, whose inability to form stable coalitions helped the Romans to extend the bounds of their Empire. 'Fortune can give no greater boon than discord among our foes,' wrote Tacitus, praying that the tribes might retain their traditional hatred one for another.

The presence of iron-using Celtic-speaking peoples in Scotland can be inferred from the seventh century BC. The evidence for this Celtic population is largely that of their fortifications, for it is to them that we can attribute many (though by no means all) of the Scottish hill-forts, whether stone-walled or with earthen ramparts and ditches. The constructional details, and the techniques of defence, used in these forts, together with the scanty finds from within them, confirm this impression. Except for a few large hill-top enclosures, most of the Scottish hill-forts which can be attributed to pre-Roman times can only represent the stronghold of petty chieftains within the framework of a fragmented Celtic society.

The earlier series of forts embody the defensive principle of a vertical sheer-faced wall fronting the enemy. To obtain such a wall, and to enable it to withstand frontal attack, the continental Celts had evolved the constructional technique of lacing the rampart of stones or earth with vertical and horizontal timber beams. In Scotland, with abundant stone available, fine timber-laced walls could be built, but they had a fatal defect. The beam ends projected from, or at least were visible flush with the outer wall-face, and offered a point of weakness in that they could be set on fire by the attacking force (101, 176). Once started, such a fire on a windy Scottish hill-top would spread roaring through the interstices of the stonework as the timber ignited and burnt to glowing charcoal, and since many of the rocks in the regions of these forts fuse at a comparatively low temperature, the whole wall would come slumping down in a semi-molten mass of vitrified blocks slagged together. These timber-laced defences which in antiquity suffered this mode of attack survive today under the name of vitrified forts, as visible evidence of their original construction, but where such burning has not taken place, excavation alone will reveal the true nature of the rampart construction.

This means, of course, that the occurrence of vitrified forts may mean nothing more than an accidental combination of circumstances involving attack by fire in areas of fusible rock,

and give no clue to the original distribution of the technique of timber-laced fort walls in Scotland. And again, there is every reason to think that once established, this technique continued to be employed for some centuries, well into the post-Roman period. But, using the evidence of wall construction and of associated finds we can see that in the north and west timber-laced forts are likely to have been built from the eighth century B C, particularly in the Borders, and that forts with sheer-faced stone walls belong to the same story.

Apart from vitrified forts and other stone-built structures, loosely grouped as duns and which may be of any date up to and within the earlier Middle Ages, the main concentration of hill-forts of types broadly comparable with those of the rest of Britain (and especially of southern England) is south of the Forth-Clyde line, and more particularly among the foothills of the Cheviots, in the valley of the Tweed and in tributaries, a concentration which extends into Northumberland. It must be remembered that these forts are small in comparison with many in Wessex and Sussex, and that the northern midlands of England has nothing comparable.

The earliest series of Scottish hill-forts, as we have seen, should belong to the eighth century B C, and, as elsewhere in Britain, be in origin an indigenous development. Later we see a change in defensive tactics in Scotland – the use of defence in depth, with more than one line of rampart or wall, and the use of steeply sloping bank-and-ditch systems rather than sheer-faced walls. Such modifications took place during a period of technological change from bronze to iron for edge-tools, but the two developments need not necessarily be related.

At more than one fort one can see that the earlier wall construction has been modified to make the sloping rampart-and-ditch defences. At best there are few finds to be associated with the forts; at times nothing has survived except the ruined defences themselves. The stone-built hut foundations to be seen in so many of these forts all seem to be secondary structures built after the fort had gone out of active use. It seems

Abernethy, Perthshire: timber-laced wall, Iron Age fort (above); Kidlaw, East Lothian: rampart and ditch (below)

possible that there was no permanent occupation in the smaller forts at least, and that they must be regarded as strongholds and places of refuge for use in emergency. Like all barbarian warfare, that of the Celts was essentially a matter of raids and skirmishes, of tip-and-run attacks and sudden unpredictable changes of intention: one cannot regard the hill-forts as designed to withstand sieges even on the small mediaeval scale.

As far as actual settlements go, we have evidence that both the single steading and the nucleated group of up to fifteen or more houses were in use in Scotland at this time, and on into the period of the Roman occupation. House plans, as elsewhere in Britain, were circular, and the construction was of timber uprights and wattle-and-daub walling. Hayhope Knowe, a settlement in the Cheviots, probably originally comprised some fifteen or more houses each about 10 m in dia-

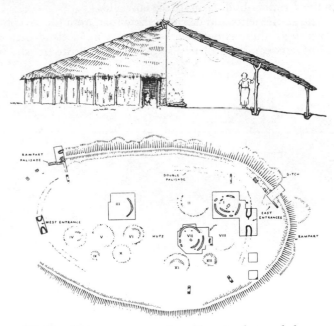

Hayhope Knowe: reconstruction of Iron Age hut, and plan; Peebles: Orchard Rig settlement (facing)

meter, enclosed with a palisade; later a scare caused the in-habitants to begin to surround their village with a ditch and timber-faced rampart, but this was never completed. Single steadings in Stirlingshire and Fife have houses from 12 m to 20 m in diameter, standing in enclosed farm yards up to 45 m across. In some districts these single-steading farms were set in bogs or on lake sides to form the type of structure called a crannog. Such crannogs continued to be built well into the Middle Ages, and many of the Scottish examples are of late date, but some in the south-west, in Ayrshire and Galloway, were substantial timber-framed circular houses with a central hearth, and diameters of 12 m to 20 m and dated from the fifth century BC. In the Islands and Highlands the circular stone-built structures of the types known as brochs and wheelhouses repeat in essentials the details of planning already established in these timber-built farms of the Lowlands.

The settlements and defences show that, from the seventh century BC there is evidence of a society in Scotland with a ruling aristocracy, probably speaking Gallo-Brittonic, and a

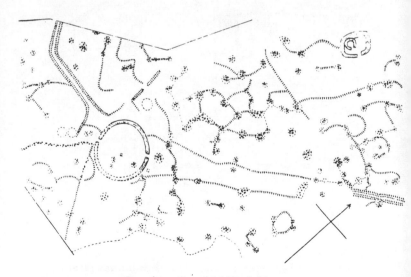

Dumfries: Stanshiel Rig field system

knowledge of fortification techniques and house and farm-stead types current elsewhere in Britain. We know of a few of their personal trinkets and possessions together with their iron tools and weapons, the first to be seen in Scotland. The use of iron for edge-tools meant a great advance in technology, for iron is an abundant and therefore cheap metal, and tools made from it are highly effective. Without iron axes it is hardly conceivable that the timber-work needed for forts and farm-steads could have been provided.

The building of even the smaller Scottish forts must have involved no mean amount of labour. This would have been the case more particularly in the instance of the timber-laced forts, where not only had stone to be collected and built into the defensive walls, but a considerable amount of timber selected and cut down. It has been calculated that for one of the small-est of the timber-laced forts that we know, at Abernethy (227) in Perthshire, an absolute minimum of 1,000 linear m of tim-ber of 230 mm scantling would be required, which would have involved the felling of some 640 young trees, which under natural conditions would be scattered through about 24 ha of woodland. This estimate only allows for a defensive wall 1.5 m high, and double the figures is really much more probable. Similar figures can be obtained from other timber-built struc-tures, such as the settlements of circular timber-framed huts enclosed by stockades or palisades which we have just dis-cussed. At Hayhope Knowe, in Roxburghshire, the enclosing palisade contained 1,600 posts of 200 mm scantling, together with hurdle work approximating to the yield of 3.6 ha of coppice, exclusive of the uprights and wattle-work of the houses. The crannog structures utilised enormous quantities of timber, both as upright piles and as foundations and flooring beams, quite apart from roofing poles and the woodwork of the approach causeway.

We have then to consider communities by now well equipped with iron tools and with considerable skill in do-mestic and military architecture in timber work and stone. While corn was certainly ground with querns of the rotary and 'saddle' type, there is little evidence of the intensive system of fields tilled with the traction-plough in southern Britain until

Roman times. Archaeology confirms the evidence of the classical writers that corn-growing may have played a relatively
small part in the economy of North Britain at the time of the
Roman Conquest, and indeed it might be reasonable to accept
Dio's statement about the tribes of north-east Scotland, who,
although they went to battle with a chariot force, nevertheless
had neither permanent settlements nor stable agriculture, but
were pastoralists and food-gatherers.

Such an economy, however, in no way precludes the posses-
sion of considerable wealth, or the development of the crafts of
carpenter, wheelwright, blacksmith and worker in fine metals.
Indeed communities of this type are favourable to the growth
of a warrior aristocracy which can assure a patronage for the
craftsman engaged on the production of weapons and engines
of war, of chariots, of trappings and parade ornaments for men
and horses, and of luxury goods for the household and women-
folk of the noble families. A chieftain's duties include hospi-
tality, and great bronze cauldrons, hung by elaborate wrought-
iron chains above the central hearth of the house, show how
the tradition of the Cauldron of Abundance and the Champion's Portion, familiar in the Irish tales, is a real thing, with
its roots deep in prehistory. We think too of cauldrons elsewhere in the ancient world, and remember how, as in Classical
Greece, they could so often be symbolic objects dedicated in
temples and sanctuaries: the Cimbri sent a votive cauldron,
the most sacred in their country, as a present to Augustus. On
the other hand, although the wainwright could and did devote
his skill to building chariots, the farm cart with clumsy, nearly
solid wheels made of three planks jointed together was also in
use at this time as it was in earlier centuries.

Compared with the rest of the British Isles, Scotland has
produced relatively few pieces of fine parade equipment in
bronze and iron of the immediately pre-Roman centuries, or
within the period of the Roman occupation. But those that
survive show how the extraordinary art-style, evolved among
the Continental Celts from the fifth century BC onwards, ran a
vigorous course in Britain after the Roman occupation of the
main Celtic areas of the European mainland had led to its
extinction there. The British craftsmen developed the Conti-

nental styles, based on classical and even oriental motifs, and blended them into a strange compelling art of pattern and in-direct imagery, rather than of representation, and produced a series of insular schools which could at their best create works of art of the highest order. A bronze horse-cap, part of the parade equipment of a warrior's pony, from Torrs in Galloway, is among the finest pieces of the earlier schools in Britain, and may date from the end of the third century BC – if so, it and the bird-headed horned terminals found with it may be evidence of the precocious establishment of such traditions in south-west Scotland. Minor pieces in bronze from Scotland include scab-bards for the slender iron swords of the Celts, mountings of long wooden shields, fair-leads for reins, the snaffle-bits of chariot ponies, and a mirror for a lady of high estate. A bronze boar's head from Banffshire is likely to have been the mouth-piece of a Celtic war trumpet or carnyx, the braying of which, coupled with the warcry or what Tacitus recorded as the *bar-ritus*, must have served to augment the confusion and carnage on many a battlefield.

Fighting was by sword, spear and sling: the bow and arrow were not used by the Celtic warrior. The war-chariot, drawn by a pair of ponies and carrying a driver and a warrior, was built for lightness and strength and in effect nothing but a tiny metre-square platform, open front and back, and with side screens alone, on a pair of spoked wheels with iron tires. The horses were clearly bred for the task, and highly trained, and the virtuosity of the charioteers confronting Caesar in south-east England in the first century BC drew a tribute from that sur-prised and somewhat discomfited Roman general. For he had not expected these tactics, since chariot warfare was not used by the Continental Celts against the Roman army in Gaul: the use of chariots against the Severan campaigns in Scotland in the second century AD is the last recorded appearance of this Celtic war-engine.

Among personal adornments there are great heavy bronze armlets, which seem to have been a speciality of north-east Scotland in the second century AD, and snake bracelets recall-ing one found near Cambridge in a Belgic chieftain's grave of the early first century AD. Gold was used for even more splen-

did objects, such as the great torc or neck ornament of which a fragment was found in Peeblesshire, and which closely resembles gold torcs from East Anglia – another instance of the relations between Scotland and southern England at this time. With the torc fragment were found gold coins of a Gaulish tribe, but these, and others from Lanarkshire, must have been regarded as bullion, and could never have been in circulation, for coinage was not in use in the north at this time.

We know from the classical writers that objects in precious metals were dedicated by the Celts in the sanctuaries of their gods, and the torc, insignia of royalty, is seen on many a carving of Gaulish deities. Such representations in stone or wood must have existed in Britain as elsewhere in the Celtic world, and it is not too fanciful to imagine some of the massive and heavy torcs, hanging as votive offerings on the necks of images carved in the strange and terrifying manner of the barbarian artist and recalling not only the tree-trunk deities of the Gauls described by Lucan, but those of post-Roman Britain seen and shunned by Gildas. Indeed, we have a find from Ballachulish which may well be of pre-Roman age. It is an oaken image of a woman 1.5 m high, her eyes of inlaid quartz pebbles, and it was found beneath peat in what appears to have been the remains of a wattled hut or shrine. Of course the figure may be of any pre-Christian period, but there are reasons which make one connect it with somewhat similar north German and east English finds which seem likely to belong to the early centuries AD.

The evidence of archaeology and of literary sources also go together to show that the Celts had sanctuary sites of more than one kind, including sacred pools into which offerings were placed on ceremonial occasions. Three finds from southern Scotland, of collections of metal tools and weapons, found, in two instances, within bronze cauldrons in bogs or lakes, seem only explicable in this way: perhaps the custom of depositing 'bog butter' may date from this time. But what the Middle Sanctuary of the south Scottish Celts was, which has come down in a Romanised place-name as *Medionemeton*,

Deskford, bronze carnyx (above); Culbin Sands, armlet (below)

somewhere near the Antonine Wall, we do not yet know.

Let us now try to put together the various pieces of evidence, and see what description we can give of the land and people of prehistoric Scotland at the moment of entering the phase of written history when the Roman military forces arrived in AD 80. What manner of men and what conditions did Agricola encounter? To answer this question we can use not only the evidence of archaeology, but that of the classical writers, of the Irish oral tradition committed to writing in early mediaeval times, of the survival of Celtic institutions down to the same period, and inferences from comparative philology.

Though, over the space of three thousand years, an appreciable amount of natural woodland would have been cleared by agriculture or grazing, great tracts of the landscape must still have been heavily wooded, in areas where now there stretches bog or moorland, as well as in what is today arable and settled land. The chariot warfare, which we know the Celts to have practised in Scotland as elsewhere, implies the existence of areas of at least relatively open parkland to allow for such chariot manoeuvres to have taken place, even if some of the forest clearance was caused by grazing rather than by cultivation.

When considering the population we must remember that, although at least a ruling class of Celtic-speaking peoples was established in many regions of Scotland by the first century AD, this did not mean the extermination of the previous inhabitants, whose ancestry went back to the days of Cairnpapple and Skara Brae, and to the fishers and boatmen of Oronsay or the Forth shore. Linguistically, for instance, the Gallo-Brittonic dialects could have existed side by side with other tongues now wholly unknown and perhaps numerous and varied – the Australian aborigines, some 200,000 strong when first discovered, were speaking more than 500 languages and dialects. Out of the 38 native names recorded in Scotland in the second century AD by the geographer Ptolemy, only 42 per cent are certainly or probably Celtic. As usual, it is the names of natural features which survive the longest – only 35 per cent of these are Celtic, as against the 53 per cent among

78

the names of tribes and settlement centres. It must of course be borne in mind in this context that we are only concerned with that branch of the Celtic language of which the main descendant is Welsh, for there is no evidence that the other branch, represented by Scottish Gaelic, existed here until its introduction by the Scotti from Ulster in the fifth century AD.

Of the organisation and structure of society in the non-Celtic areas we have no knowledge, but within the areas under Celtic rule – and that may well have been most of habitable Scotland in the first century AD – we can see something of the likely social pattern. There existed some fifteen or so major tribes – Smertae, Damnonii, Votandini and the rest – each governed by a ruler with the status of a tribal chieftain or a *basileus* of Hesiod's Dark Age Greece. Such tribal leaders in southern Britain were on occasions of special relationships described by the Romans as *rex*, and they seem to have held office by reason of their membership of the ruling house. They could indeed be men or women, as Cartimanndua of the Brigantes and Boudica of the Iceni give witness.

Within the tribe a socially stratified society linked the classes one to another by obligation and land tenure. Settlement seems to have been based largely on the individual steading, but these may have been grouped into what in recent times became called the 'township' or baile, the same grouping of households with collectively tilled common fields and communally owned pasture and grazing. The free men of the settlement (on historical analogies) could have owned shares in the common land, and it seems likely, again on comparative historical evidence, that the skilled craftsmen, whether bards or blacksmiths, would also have their rights there. But between the chieftain and the commoners there came a class of nobles or barons or thanes, a warrior aristocracy, the *equites* of Caesar, who in Ireland at least, and most likely elsewhere in the British Isles, specifically counted their wealth in cattle and whose individual allotment of arable or grazing was a separate portion not included in the common lands of the settlement. These were the men who fought from the chariot, rather than on foot like the lower classes of freemen; these, too, with the chieftain were probably the main owners of slaves who had not the rights of the freemen of the society. Chieftain and nobles formed a general assembly denoted in the Indo-European languages by various names indicating 'the whole' (in Irish, the word for 'tribe'), and although the ruler came from a royal family, it seems that his succession had at least to be formally ratified by the assembly.

We know that the priestly caste, the druids, were of great importance in the Celtic world, but their precise status in the social hierarchy, as far as land tenure is concerned, is obscure. It seems likely that bards and magicians, as a privileged class would be entitled to separate allocations of land, and in later times in Ireland this was certainly the case.

The pattern of the Celtic tribes was therefore that of agreed areas under individual rule (though doubtless the boundaries were often in dispute). Below the chieftain came the nobility, the 'Cow Lords' and charioteers, with their individual allocations of land; below them again the free men of the settlement with their common land. All classes were bound by obligations and allegiance, and the General Assembly of the king and his nobles determined political and military action. Inter-tribal warfare, and petty skirmishes between factious nobles and their followers, seem to have been constant. Some at least of the Celtic warriors fought naked, doubtless in consonance with some religious sanction, and many tribes and regions had the custom of painting or tattooing their bodies. Head-hunting played an important part in such activities, the heads of the victims being carried home in triumph on the chariot and preserved in the house or impaled over the gate of the hill-fort; cattle raiding was an honourable and accepted occupation for a gentleman.

It is against such a background then that we must set Calgacus, the Swordsman as his name tells us, the first man in Scotland whose name we know. He and his nobles, like their Gaulish cousins described so vividly by Diodorus Siculus, no doubt shaved their faces but 'let their moustaches grow so long that their mouths are covered up; and so when they eat, these get entangled in the food, while their drink is taken in, as it were, through a strainer.' They too would wear the Celtic dress that so astonished the classical world – 'amazing clothes, shirts with flowing patterns and dyed all kinds of colours and trousers called *brakai*; perhaps, too, as Diodorus noted, in speech they may have been 'sparing of words and enigmatical,' though 'boastful, threatening and braggarts by nature.' Ceremonial feasting would take place in the big circular thatched house, with the guests graded according to status as they sat round the central hearth with the bubbling cauldron of boiled pork; behind each warrior would stand his armour-bearer, and to the bravest warrior went the choicest joint, the Champion's Portion. Beer or mead would be brought to the guests by a servant moving sun-wise, just as the port decanter circulates today.

It is a barbarous society that we reconstruct, not far from that of Dark Age Greece reflected in Homer, nearer perhaps to that of Beowulf, preserving the texture and idiom of the earlier Indo-European institutions in the same sense that the Celtic languages retain the features that relate them to earlier dialects. For the Romans who had absorbed the Oriental and Mediterranean civilities, an incomprehensible order of things: on the frontiers of their Empire they were separated from their opponents not only by a physical, but by a moral and psychological barrier across which understanding could not reach. The Celtic peoples could not achieve the concept of unity even among themselves, let alone conceive of a world containing both Celts and Romans. 'Seldom is it,' wrote Tacitus of the Britons, 'that two or three states meet together to ward off a common danger. Thus, while they fight singly, all are conquered.' And as a modern historian discussing this very problem has said, 'the conduct of the barbarians was rendered worse by the incalculable changes of their moods; they were not guided by logical and reasoned thinking but rather by sudden emotion.' On the other hand, the ancient antithesis of civilised and barbarian, the Tribes Without the Law, was as ineradicably fixed in the Roman mind as in that of Rudyard Kipling. Neither philosophically nor juridically did Roman thought admit the possibility of 'good barbarians,' unless they were firmly under the contractual obligations of a client kingdom or incorporated within the Empire. It was a spiritual and moral as well as a political impasse, and in Scotland, on the outer rim even of Celtic culture, perhaps more impossible of solution than elsewhere in western Europe.

The Roman occupation of Scotland was, like that of the rest of the Highland Zone of Britain, a military garrison established among people of alien traditions, at a lower stage of technological capacity, and with at best a rudimentary and often savage code of law and government. In the face of such an occupying force, determined to preserve peace in the regions it controlled and to put an end to the eternal quarrels and raids between rival families, clans and tribes, that were the breath of life to the Celtic warrior, three main courses of action were open to the barbarians. In the first place, it was possible for a native tribe to accept Roman rule, even to welcome it; such an arrangement could be advantageous to both sides and could either be an informal state of non-aggression, or could be ratified by appropriate legal machinery. In the south of Scotland it looks as though the tribes of the Damnonii and the Votadini took such a course at an early stage of the occupation.

A second (and perhaps the most usual) relationship between native and Roman was that of keeping the peace to the minimal degree consonant with reprisals, at least in the immediate neighbourhood of the garrisons or the ambit of their scouting parties. The more remote from the Roman military zone, the more lawless could the tribe be – what happened north of the Great Glen was nobody's business. But the third, and perhaps more personal, solution of the problem of co-existence of incompatible cultures, was for the ruler and his retainers to move out of reach of the military forces, and if possible to put sea or mountain between himself and them.

It is instructive, however, to look first at the situation in the heavily garrisoned area between Hadrian's and the Antonine Walls, especially that part of it in which, as we saw earlier, the builders of hill-forts had established themselves. This was the region in part within the tribal areas of the Votadini and the Damnonii who, as we have said, seem to have come to terms with the occupying forces, and in part within that of the Selgovae, whose submission was probably compelled. The evidence from the hill-forts of the Border counties is eloquent enough as to what was achieved by forcible or persuasive

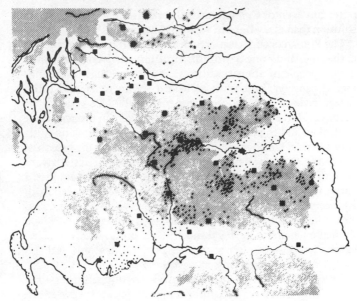

Hill-forts and Roman forts in south Scotland

Roman action. Time and time again we can trace the growth, within the defended areas, of congeries of circular stone-walled huts or small houses which, on excavation, prove to belong to the period of the Roman occupation, though some are indeed also earlier, and which not only fill the fort but sprawl over once-defensive walls and ramparts by then out of commission and half ruined. The *pax romana* was no empty phrase, whether achieved by force or by the consent of at least the tribal leaders, and the clan warfare and cattle-raids of which the forts are the archaeological expression could not be tolerated in Romanised territory. Once rallying places of the war-bands, the forts could still have remained the high places of tribal prestige and tradition, but as civil settlements. The nucleation of settlement they presuppose may have been accompanied by, and be in part the outcome of, improved agricultural techniques introduced by the Romans in an attempt to increase local corn production: certainly Romano-

Celtic tools of southern English types appear at this time in the Scottish Lowlands.

It was a Celtic custom to have periodic tribal or religious assemblies at fixed places, not necessarily at any permanent settlement, where ceremonies could take place, laws be promulgated, and a fair or market held. Such meetings may have been recognised, within the Roman provinces, as lawful and permissible. We have seen too how there were sanctuaries such as Medionemeton somewhere near the Antonine Wall, while the votive offerings made in lakes must not be forgotten.

A place named in a Roman source as that of Maponus lay within the tribe of the Novantae, whose territory seems to have stretched from the River Nith into Galloway: Maponus was a Celtic god of youth, music and markets, and Lochmaben may preserve his name. It was against the Novantae and the Selgovae that Agricola directed his attack at an early stage of his campaign in AD 82. During the next two years he was engaged in the combined operations in eastern Scotland which culminated in the engagement at Mons Graupius. These campaigns, or the impending threat of such events, would have forced upon the Celtic tribes the alternative courses of action we have mentioned – submission, real or superficial, or withdrawal to regions out of reach of the Roman army.

In such a context it is interesting to consider the Western Isles within the first couple of centuries AD. In the third millennium BC they had supported a population of stone-using agriculturalists whose enduring memorial is their chambered collective tombs. After this episode there is virtually no evidence of anything but the most scanty and sparse settlement, often of none at all, until there appear the abundant remains of the stone-built houses, byres and farmsteads of iron-using farmers, and the circular defensive tower-houses known as brochs. Once established, such structures were built and lived in for several centuries, into the post-Roman Dark Ages.

The material equipment of the settlers would be perfectly in accord with their having origins on the mainland. The circular

Sollas, N. Uist: wheelhouse (above);
Quanterness, Orkney: round house, c. 500 BC (below)

stone houses are no more than local versions of the timber-built farmsteads which we have already noticed, adapted to conditions of scanty wood and an inclement climate; bone weaving tools and other objects imply sheep farmers making woollen cloth according to traditional techniques widespread in immediately pre-Roman Britain and well represented from West Yorkshire to Galloway.

The structure called a wheel-house, from its plan with radial stone piers representing the wooden posts of the prototype, is clearly the Hebridean equivalent of the farmhouse unit or single steading which we have seen to have been typical of the immediately pre-Roman agrarian economy over most of the British mainland. The animal bones from such houses, and tools such as the weaving-combs mentioned above, show that the builders were farmers grazing sheep for wool – their stock, and any seed corn they may have possessed, must have been taken to the islands during the immigration. The same economy lies behind the brochs, but these remarkable structures show a peculiarly Scottish development whereby the circular stone-walled house was turned into a defensive tower (see Index of Sites). Much is still obscure about the precise manner in which these tower-houses, some at least built to a height of 6 m or more, were roofed or floored internally, and there is likely to have been considerable individual variation; but one thing is clear. We are dealing with a development exactly analogous to the evolution of the mediaeval peel or tower-house in North Britain, and presumably the result of similar circumstances – insecurity, clan or tribal warfare, cattle thieving and family feuds. It is possible that the broch builders felt the need to defend themselves against an enemy more dreaded than their own kinsfolk, the power of the Roman military forces, which, as Agricola's circumnavigation of Scotland showed, could strike by sea as well as by land. Was this act indeed a demonstration directed *in terrorem* to show that even those in the Islands were not necessarily out of reach?

In the event, there is no evidence that punitive measures were ever taken against these settlements. In fact, it looks as though some peaceable trading took place between the Roman world and the Hebridean crofters, and that the woollen industry of the north, as elsewhere in the Roman Province, was encouraged as a deliberate piece of economic policy. The Celtic north and west was moving towards the place it was to occupy in the earliest Middle Ages, when the movements of peoples in the immemorial manner of prehistory were to begin again, for the Roman grip on northern Europe had become relaxed and ineffective. With the arrival of the Scotti from Ulster in the fifth century AD and the later Anglian settlement in the south-east, historical Scotland with its amalgam of prehistoric traditions of language and culture, mingled with those of Irish and Germanic origins, began to take shape.

Lewis: Carloway broch

V

We have brought the story of the beginnings of Scotland to a point where historical record, coupled with the evidence of archaeology, leads us to a new world. But how new? What of the contributions to the pattern of early historic and mediaeval Scotland made by the anonymous peoples of the prehistoric past? As we have seen, for a period of at least seven thousand years before Agricola, Scotland had been an area of settlement, migration, conflict and change, never for long isolated from the movements of peoples and the interchange of ideas which affected the whole European continent. The change from a prehistoric to an historic state of affairs is after all something of an accident, perceptible to us as students of the past but of little or no consequence to most of the population at the time. The historical components of early Scotland – Picts, Scots, Anglians and Norsemen – are social or political entities with written labels attached to them, but in no other way different from the makers of beaker pottery or of hill-forts with timbered walls whose tribal names have not survived to be recorded in written form. Nor did the prehistoric inhabitants of

Scotland differ from ourselves or our historical ancestors in appearance, however alien and remote their thoughts and emotions.

If we now turn to what was new and what was old in early historic Scotland, we should remind ourselves at the outset that the basic structure of agrarian life as it continued in north-western Europe until the eve of the Industrial Revolution (and indeed survived in remote areas, such as the Hebrides, until yesterday), was formed by the beginning of the Christian era, and had its roots deep in the fourth millennium BC. For the simpler techniques of fishing by line or net or fish-trap we must indeed look to an even more ancient world, that of the surviving traditions of the Stone Age. To these traditions, too, certainly go back the skills of dressing and working skins, leather and pelts, and probably the concept of the tailored garments which, in alien materials, are today sometimes (rather pathetically) conceived of as the hall-mark of the Western technocrat. And as regards transport, it is again to these remote times that we can attribute the first use of boats and sledges.

The basic techniques of mixed farming, combining flocks and herds with the cultivation of a cereal crop, had been introduced into Scotland, as into the rest of the British Isles, in the centuries centred on 4000 BC, and were developed and modified to a stage beyond that of the simple croft before the advent of the Romans. The basic crops of wheat and four-rowed barley or bere were being grown in Scotland early in the third millennium BC, though oats and rye seem an introduction of the Roman period: man does not live by bread alone, and the distinction between bread corn and drink corn, explicit in the Celtic world of the last few centuries BC, was already ancient at that time; so, too, was the knowledge of the alluring properties of mead.

The Highland breeds of sheep, now represented by the Soay and Orkney types, and the goats which have run wild from originally domesticated stock, may conceivably go back to the breeds first brought to Britain by the Stone Age farmers, and certainly to those bred by pre-Roman Celts; to the latter again we can attribute the old Scottish dark brindled (or 'black') cattle, and the ponies of Shetland and allied breeds. And with the sheep goes the woollen industry, which as practised by Highland crofters up to the present time is hardly, if at all, modified from that of the builders of the brochs. Indeed, the whole structure of the pre-industrial agrarian economy, and with it the basic rural technology of carpenter, wheelwright and blacksmith, potter, thatcher and hurdle-maker, could be said to have been fully formed at the advent of Agricola.

More too than this. The crofting pattern based on township, inbye and pasture, remains the tangible expression of an ancient social pattern, and characteristically that of the Celts. In the Highlands and Islands this structure was reinforced in early historical times by the coming of the Scots from Ulster. While their variant of Celtic was not that hitherto spoken in Scotland, they were basically members of the common Celtic social order, and would have encountered nothing new in the way of life of the Celts already established in those regions. Even in the areas of Anglian settlement it must be remembered that the Germanic tribes too were heirs to a long-standing tradition, with an agrarian economy differing little in its basic structure from that of the Celts. To these people, however, and to the Norsemen, there belongs the tradition of the rectangular house-plan, a tradition which was completely to supplant the ancient Celtic (and pre-Celtic) circular form.

In those realms of human culture that do not leave their trace in the archaeological record, or at best may survive only in ambiguous and indirect evidence, we can least of all perceive survival or innovation. Music and the dance, the tale and the poem, the beliefs and the concepts of ancient man, are of all things the most elusive, even where writing is available. So often we are faced with what has been called conditional literacy, where a script and a language (as for instance Latin during the Roman occupation of Britain) is used only for restricted and formal purposes. When there is an oral literary tradition for works of the imagination (and even for such factual information as a genealogy) this stands side by side with the technique of writing, and does not use it as a means of record: it has no need to, for the technique of oral transmission, carefully acquired and fostered, already serves this purpose. The Gaelic oral tradition is of course in origin an Irish one, and we will now never know what hero-tales may have been recited round the hearth of broch or wheel-house, crannog or lowland homestead in pre-Roman, pre-Gaelic, but still Celtic, Scotland.

But who can tell from what deep well of tradition many of the half-expressed fears and traditional beliefs of the countryside may be drawn, how far back into prehistory their roots may stretch? It was at the beginning of this century that the weathered limb-bone of a whale, its half-human shape improved to form a face, was found on Bernera by a crofter who thought it to be one of the old gods of the island fraught with ill-luck. It was given to a visitor, whose return journey was a tale of troubles, the whale-bone image only being accepted as a passenger by the boatman after protest and its concealment in a sack, and on the mainland it was hysterically denied accommodation with its owner in the hotel. It was still an object of terror: its date is unknown, and it could belong to any period. It is somehow symbolic, as timeless as the traditions and fears with which it was so lately endowed.

Towie: stone ball

GAZETTEER OF MONUMENTS

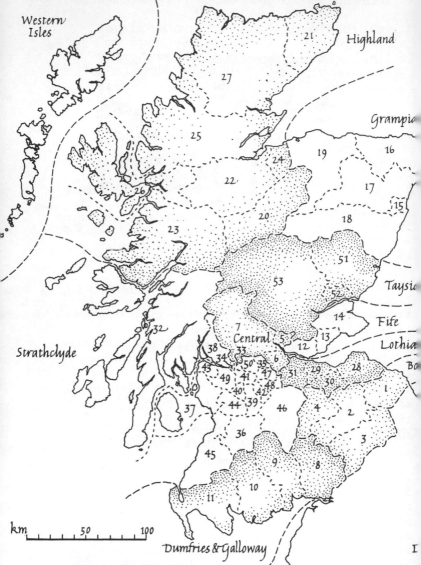

Western
Isles

Highland

21

27

Grampia

25

19

16

24

17

22

15

26

20

18

23

51

Taysi

53

52

32

14

Fife

7

Central

5

12

13

Lothia

38

33

6

28

Bo

34

50

39

31

29

Strathclyde

43

49

41

47

1

30

40

48

42

44

39

46

4

2

37

36

3

45

9

8

10

11

Dumfries & Galloway

I

km

50

100

Scotland. Regions and Districts (excluding Orkney and Shetland)

Districts not listed in the Gazetteer are printed in *italic*

GAZETTEER

The prehistoric monuments of Scotland are vivid reminders of man's ancient past, and the remarkable state of preservation of many of them is equalled only by their locations amid unspoilt scenery. The range and variety of the monuments is unrivalled in Europe, and for many areas, particularly in the Highlands, it has been difficult to decide what to exclude, and to choose a small number of representative examples from the rich store of visible remains. Any selection of sites is a subjective one, but examples of some of the best-preserved, most dramatic or merely typical field-monuments in Scotland have been included; the intention has been to mirror the first part of this volume and to illustrate the range of monuments studied by prehistorians and thus to evoke a general response from their examination rather than to provide a detailed assessment of individual sites.

This gazetteer is organised by the present administrative divisions into nine Regions and three Islands Authorities, with the Districts in alphabetical order within each Region; within each District the sites are arranged alphabetically by place-name. The Districts are also identified by a number which refers to the map on p.94. The gazetteer includes all the prehistoric sites in the care of the Secretary of State for Scotland as well as many others on private ground; the intending visitor must always seek the permission of the landowner or farmer before walking to a site and must check that he has parked his car in a way that does not impede the work of the estate or farm. Lambing, growing crops or shooting may make it impossible to visit some sites at certain times of the year. Visitors should always follow the Country Code and keep to paths whenever possible. Where there is a recent and authoritative local guide-book, which includes monuments in the guardianship of the Secretary of State for Scotland (e.g. Arran, Grampian, Orkney), fewer details are provided, although the main sites in the area are listed. Armed with the Ordnance Survey 1:50,000 map the visitor will be able to add many further sites to his itinerary; for this reason detailed instructions about access have not been provided, as it is possible to approach many sites in several ways. Some well-preserved sites have, however, been excluded because of problems of access for a variety of reasons.

The entries are based on personal visits, the Inventories of the Royal Commission on the Ancient and Historical Monuments of Scotland, and on the Record Cards of the former Archaeology Division of the Ordnance Survey.

The name and the type of the site are followed by the National Grid Reference, the Ordnance Survey 1:50,000 sheet number and details of how the site is identified on the map; in only a few cases are sites not pinpointed on the os map.

The sites held in trust for posterity by the Secretary of State for Scotland and cared for on his behalf by the Scottish Development Department (Ancient Monuments Branch) are indicated by the abbreviation sDD, and the hours of admission are indicated. In most cases admission is at any reasonable time without charge, while in others a key must be obtained from a place close to a site; in a few cases there is a permanent custodian and at these sites the opening hours are standard:

From 1 April–30 September Weekdays 9.30 am–7 pm
                                    Sundays 2 pm–7 pm
From 1 October–31 March Weekdays 9.30 am–4 pm
                                    Sundays 2 pm–4 pm

The hours are, however, subject to revision, and exigencies of staffing may mean that a monument may sometimes be closed.

BORDERS

1.   COCKBURN LAW
     Cairn and Fort NT 765597, sh 67, Fort
There are the remains of a cairn around the OS triangulation station on the summit of Cockburn Law; the summit area is the site of a fort which measures about 110 m by 85 m internally, and has up to three lines of defence. There are superb views of the Merse from the summit.

2.   DIRRINGTON GREAT LAW
     Cairns NT 698549, sh 67, not marked
Two large cairns stand on opposite sides of a smaller cairn on the summit of the hill; the westernmost, which is the largest, measures 17 m in diameter by almost 2 m in height, and is surrounded by an irregular ditch.

3.   DIRRINGTON LITTLE LAW
     Cairn NT 686530, sh 67, not marked
The substantial cairn on the summit of the hill is about 20 m in diameter and 2 m high.

4.   EARN'S HEUGH
     Forts NT 892691, sh 67, Forts
These two forts, which are situated adjacent to each other at the edge of the spectacular sea-cliffs on the hill known as Tun Law, are approached on foot from Westside Farm. Within the defences of the NW fort, there is a stone-walled settlement, itself overlain by a settlement of nine stone-walled houses. The SE fort has a complex series of ramparts which in some cases join the two forts together. The site was excavated by Professors V.G.Childe and C.Daryll Forde in 1931; the meagre finds are in the National Museum of Antiquities of Scotland, Edinburgh.

5.   EDIN'S HALL
     Fort, Broch and Settlement NT 772603,
     sh 67, Fort and Broch
Situated on the NE flank of Cockburn Law on the N edge of a broad sweep of the Whiteadder Water, the broch is one of the best preserved of southern Scotland. It stands within the W half of an earlier fort, which is defended by two ramparts and ditches and measures about 135 m by 75 m internally; at least two periods of fort construction may be detected. The E half of the fort is occupied by a settlement of stone-walled houses, some of which overlie the defences. The complete base of the

broch survives, its walls still standing to a height of 2 m. The interior measures about 17 m in diameter, and it is thus much larger in internal area than most of the northern brochs with which it may otherwise be compared, but it is perhaps unlikely that the broch reached any considerable height. The entrance-passage, which is on the E side of the broch, is checked for a door rather more than halfway along its length, and there is a guard-cell on either side with the openings behind the door. Within the thickness of the broch wall and opening from the N, W and S sides are three cells, the latter providing access to a stair, which formerly led to the wall-head. In the latter half of the 18th century the site was known as Wooden's Hall and it is likely that the present name is derived from Woden or Odin.

s d d : all times without charge.

5

6. HABCHESTER
   Fort NT 944587, sh 67, Fort
Situated at the W end of Lamberton Moor overlooking Ayton, this fort measures about 100 m by 80 m internally; the defences comprise a pair of ramparts and ditches, but only the S E side of the fort is still well preserved.

7. MUTINY STONES
   Long Cairn NT 622590, sh 67, Long Cairn

This impressive long cairn is situated in moorland above the valley of the Dye Water, a little over 1 km NNW of Byrecleugh. Aligned ENE and WSW, it is about 80 m long and stands to a height of 2.5 m at its ENE end. It was excavated in 1871 and 1924 without conclusive result.

2. Ettrick and Lauderdale District

8. ADDINSTON
   Fort NT 523536, sh 73, Fort

This magnificent fort is situated to the NNE of Addinston, about 1.5 m E of Carfraemill; defended by two massive ramparts with external ditches, it is one of the best-preserved earthwork monuments in Scotland.

9. BELL HILL
   Fort NT 498286, sh 73, Fort

On the E side of Bell Hill on a steep rocky ridge there are the remains of a small rectangular fort (measuring 70 m by 29 m internally) defended by three ramparts with medial ditches; there are entrances at the s and E angles.

10. BORROWSTOUN RIG
    Stone Circle NT 557523, sh 73, Stone Circle

This carefully-laid out egg-shaped ring of 32 stones is situated on the broad summit of Borrowstoun Rig a little over 2 km NE of Burncastle; none of the stones is more than 0.6 m in height and the setting is almost hidden by heather.

11. BOW
    Broch NT 461417, sh 73, Broch

The remains of the broch stand above the A7 some 3 km s of Stow; the interior measuring about 9.5 m in diameter and the wall is about 4.6 m thick.

12. EILDON HILL NORTH
    Fort NT 555328, sh 73, Fort

The fort which occupies the NE peak of the Eildon Hills to the SE of Melrose, is one of the largest in Scotland. The most prominent ramparts, clearly visible on the aerial photographs low down the slopes of the hill, enclose an area of about 16 hectares, and represent in fact the latest of three periods of defence. The earlier ramparts, however, are poorly preserved, and are overlain by some of the 300 house-platforms that can be seen in the interior – many of them showing on the photographs as circular patches of snow. On the w tip of the summit

12

of the hill there is a Roman signal station, which was excavated in 1952–3; the use of such a signal station must be
associated with the Roman fort of Newstead (*Trimontium*)
situated below the Eildon Hills on the s bank of the River
Tweed.

13.   RINK HILL
      Fort NT 480327, sh 73, Fort
This fort stands in trees to the NE of the summit of Rink Hill;
internally measuring about 65 m by 56 m it is defended by a
wall with an outer rampart. Several stretches of the outer face
of the wall are clearly visible, and there is an entrance on the E.

14.   TORWOODLEE
      Fort and Broch NS 465384, sh 73, Fort and Broch
The broch at Torwoodlee overlies the western defences of a
fort, whose ramparts are severely denuded but are still visible
on the N and W. The wall of the broch, which is nowhere more
than 1 m high, is 5.5 m thick and the central courtyard is about
12 m in diameter. There is an entrance passage on the SE; it has
distinct door-checks, and a guard-cell on its s side. On the SW
there is a chamber within the thickness of the wall with the
remains of a stair, which presumably led to the top of the wall

or to upper galleries. Excavation in 1950 suggested that the broch was deliberately slighted, perhaps by the Roman army advancing into Scotland.

3. Roxburgh District

15.   BONCHESTER HILL
       Fort NT 595117, sh 80, Fort and Settlement; Earthworks
The remains of this fort are difficult to interpret on the ground without a plan, but the position alone makes it a site worth visiting. The earliest period of occupation is represented by a stone wall (now grass-grown) enclosing an area 100 m by 85 m (to the E of the modern wall that traverses it and to the N of a rocky scar). Two additional phases of defence are represented by further lines of earthworks. The sites of several stone-walled houses can be seen in the interior, particularly on the N side.

The unusual earthworks on a lower spur to the N of the fort (NT 596120) are also worth examining, although the date of their construction is unknown; they comprise an oval earthwork flanked by a series of annexes on the w.

16.   GREENBROUGH
       Palisaded Homestead NT 813169, sh 80, not marked
A roughly rectangular enclosure (29 m by 23 m), within which there are two timber house-sites with diameters of about 7 m, is outlined by a distinct groove 0.5 m across; elsewhere, excavation has shown that grooves such as this mark the foundation trenches for stout timber fences.

17.   HOWNAM LAW
       Fort NT 796220, sh 74, Fort
This large fort is defended by a stone wall which encloses an area of about 8.5 ha on the summit of Hownam Law, a height of 449 m OD; there is an entrance on the sw, and the interior contains at least 155 house-platforms.

18.   NINESTONE RIG
       Stone Circle NY 518973, sh 79, Stone Circle
About 265 m s of the summit of Ninestone Rig there is an oval setting of nine stones (eight upright and one fallen) measuring 7 m by 6.4 m internally.

19.   RUBERS LAW
       Fort NT 580155, sh 80, Fort
The isolated and craggy summit of Rubers Law, offering magnificent views over the surrounding country, is crowned by a series of defensive works. The outermost is a denuded rampart

on the slopes below the summit, which encloses an area of about 2.8 ha. The summit itself, and an area just below it, have been defended by stout stone walls, which incorporate dressed sandstone blocks that are undoubtedly of Roman origin. Their presence indicates a Roman structure on the hilltop – a building in such a position can only have been a signal station. A hoard of bronze vessels of Roman date, discovered on the SE side of Rubers Law, is now in Hawick Museum.

20. SHANK END
Settlement NT 767157, sh 80, Settlement
This site, chosen as an example of a settlement of Iron Age date in Roxburgh District, is situated on a spur known as Shank End, and may be approached across the Kale Water and up the steep slope above the stream. It is enclosed by a wall and measures 55 m by 40 m internally; the interior contains one circular house on the E, besides several other scoops and enclosures. A much later rectangular house overlies the perimeter of the settlement on the N and is probably associated with a later stone wall which encloses the northern third of the interior. The summit of Chatto Craig, 900 m to the N (NT 767166), is crowned by the remains of a series of stone fortifications for which a Dark Age date has been suggested.

21. WODEN LAW
Fort NT 768125, sh 80, Fort
This fort is situated on the crest of Woden Law, a prominent hill overlooking the valley of the Kale Water. That the fort was occupied for a long period is shown by the complex sequences both of its defences and of the surrounding earthworks; the ramparts of the fort were reconstructed on at least two occasions. The remarkable series of earthworks to the E and S have been variously interpreted as Roman investing works for training soldiers in siege warfare, and prehistoric farm boundaries. On the rising ground to the SE of these earthworks there is a fine example of a palisaded enclosure containing a number of timber house-sites. The Roman road known as Dere Street, one of the main routes from the south, leaves the Cheviots at this point, dropping down to the valley floor before continuing towards Newstead.

4. Tweeddale District

22. BLACK MELDON
Fort NT 206425, sh 73, Fort

The ruined stone walls of this fort enclose an area measuring 73 m by 40 m, within which the positions of at least half a dozen houses may still be detected as circular grooves about 10 m in diameter. The entrance is on the s, where there is a gap in both the main wall and an outer wall that exists on all sides except the E.

23. CADEMUIR HILL
Forts NT 224370 and 230375, sh 73, Fort; Fort

The first fort on Cademuir Hill, which is situated at the sw end of the ridge, comprises a main wall enclosing an area about 70 m by 40 m, and a series of defended terraces; there is a *chevaux de frise* along the E side of the fort designed to impede access on this flank. The summit of the hill is crowned by a large fort measuring about 210 m by 120 m within what has been a thick wall; in the interior the positions of many timber houses can still be identified.

24. DREVA
Fort and Settlement NT 126353,
sh 72, Fort and Settlement

This fort is defended by two substantial stone walls, and by a series of upright stones forming a *chevaux de frise*, which is best preserved on the sw. On the NW slopes of the hill below the fort, there is an extensive settlement of stone-walled houses and scooped out yards, with traces of an associated field-system, which are all clearly visible on the photograph.

25. NORTH MUIR
Cairn NT 105503, sh 72, Nether Cairn

This unusually well-preserved cairn measures 15 m in diameter and 3.5 m in height and is situated a little to the NW of the footpath from West Linton to Medwinbank.

26. NORTHSHIELD RINGS
Fort NT 257493, sh 73, Fort

The remains of a fort defended by three ramparts and ditches, are situated to the NE of Portmore House; two phases of construction may be identified, the earliest being the innermost rampart and ditch. On the outer lip of this ditch, there is a counterscarp bank, which appears to be overridden by the inner of the two other ramparts on the w.

24

26

27. WHITE MELDON
Cairn and Fort NT 219428, sh 73, Fort

While the defences of the fort that crowns the summit of the White Meldon are not well preserved, they are interesting as they enclose an area of about 3.6 ha, a greater area than any other fort in Tweeddale. The positions of many houses can be detected in the interior, and on the summit of the hill there is a cairn measuring about 14 m in diameter and 1 m in height.

28. WHITESIDE HILL
Fort NT 168461, sh 72, Fort

This fort encloses an area of about 0.4 ha on the summit of Whiteside Hill; at least three periods of fortification are represented, though these are difficult to disentangle without a plan. There are annexes both to the N and S of the fort, and also a detached linear earthwork in the saddle to the NE.

CENTRAL

5. Clackmannan District

29. 'CLACH-MANNAN', Clackmannan
NS 911918, sh 58, not marked

The name of Clackmannan derives from the *clach*, or stone, of Manau, which has been interpreted as a district of the tribe of Gododdin, the name of the tribe who were known in Roman times as the *Votadini*. The 'stone' has been identified with a boulder (1 m by 0.8 m and 0.4 m thick) which is now set atop a further stone outside Clackmannan Tolbooth.

6. Falkirk District

30. TAPPOCH
Broch NS 833849, sh 65, Broch

Access to this broch is now difficult because of a forestry plantation, but there is a path from the track that runs SSW from the road between Torwood and West Plean at a point about 500 m NW of Torwood. The broch is well preserved, measuring about 10 m in diameter within a wall up to 7 m thick and 2.5 m in height. The entrance passage retains the door-checks, bar-hole and recess, and is still roofed by two massive lintels. An opening in the inner wall to the S of the entrance allows access to an intra-mural stair.

28>

7. Stirling District

31. CASTLEHILL WOOD
Dun NS 750909, sh 57, not marked

This example of a dun, a small Iron Age fortification of a type more frequently found in Argyll, was excavated in 1955. Situated in a characteristic position on top of a small crag, the dun is oval on plan measuring 23 m by 15 m within a stout drystone wall. The entrance passage is on the E side and had doorchecks at a point about 1 m from the outside. Objects recovered during tne excavation suggested a 2nd-century AD date.

32. CASTLETON
Cup-and-Ring Markings NS 858884 and 857879, sh 65, not marked

Situated to the NE and SE of the farm there are seven rock outcrops decorated with cup-markings, cup-and-ring markings, as well as channels and ellipses.

33. COLDOCH
Broch NS 696981, sh 57, Broch

One of the better preserved of the lowland brochs, its wall still standing to a height of 2.4 m; it measures 9 m in diameter within a wall about 5.5 m in thickness. There are three mural cells, and a stair designed to allow access to the top of the wall.

34. HILL OF AIRTHREY
Cairn NS 796981, sh 57, Cairn, Fairy Knowe

When it was excavated in 1868, this cairn is said to have been 6.4 m high, and it still measures 18 m in diameter and over 2 m in height. Excavation revealed a central cist, covered by a mound of stones; a beaker vessel was discovered near the top of the mound, clearly a secondary deposit.

35. DUMYAT
Fort NS 832973, sh 57, not marked

This fort occupies a prominent position on the shoulder of Dumyat. A pair of outer walls cut off the W approaches, the other flanks being protected by the sheer rock faces; there is also a central stone-walled enclosure measuring 27 m by 17 m internally, which is usually assumed to be a secondary dun set within an earlier fort.

36. DUNMORE
Fort NS 605864, sh 57, Fort

On the summit of Dunmore there is a fort measuring about 160 m by 50 m within a wall some 3.5 m thick. Rocky terraces to the NE and S are protected by additional walling.

DUMFRIES AND GALLOWAY

8. Annandale and Eskdale

37. BOONIES
Settlement NY 304900, sh 79, Settlement
This well-preserved example of the settlements of Dumfries-shire measures 37 m by 30 m within a substantial bank up to 2 m in height. Over a dozen circular timber houses were un-covered in the course of excavation in 1973 and 1974 and the ways that the various house-plans overlay one another showed that they represented at least seven periods of construction. Many riverside and upland settlements of broadly similar out-line probably belong to the earlier centuries AD.

38. BURNSWARK HILL
Fort NY 185785, sh 85, Fort; Roman Camps
The spectacular massif of Burnswark Hill, which rises above Lower Annandale to a height of some 300 m, has been fortified on several occasions in the Iron Age and also appears to have been used by the Roman army for field-exercises. Excavation has shown that the earliest enclosure on the summit is repre-sented by a palisade trench at the E end of the hill. The main rampart, which encloses the whole of the summit of the hill, was built around 600 BC; it had a timber revetment at the front (and probably timber support at the back); to which a stone-built face was subsequently added to provide further support. There are three entrances on the SE side, where there is also an outer rampart, and timber-built houses were found in the interior.

On both the NW and SE slopes of the hill there are Roman camps, the latter enclosing an earlier fortlet of Antonine date at its N corner. The camps have been interpreted as the bases for Roman soldiers on field-exercises, in the course of which the Iron Age fort was used as the target for ballista attack.

39. GIRDLESTANES and LOUPIN STANES
Stone Circles NY 253961 and 257966,
sh 79, Girdlestanes; Loupin Stanes
Only the E half of the first setting survives, the W half having been destroyed by the River White Esk; eleven upright, and as many fallen, stones survive, all on the arc of a circle some 40 m in diameter. The Loupin Stanes, situated about 570 m to the NE, is an oval setting of twelve stones, measuring 10.4 m by 9.5 m, with the two tallest stones on the SW.

9. Nithsdale

40. MULLACH
Fort NX 929869, sh 78, Fort

This fort is notable for both the mass of vitrified material, which indicates the line of its timber-laced walls, and the magnificent views it offers over the surrounding area. The interior of the fort measures some 90 m by 75 m and the space between the two walls, which are unusually far apart, may have been intended to act as a stock enclosure.

41. TWELVE APOSTLES
Stone Circle NX 947794, sh 84, Twelve Apostles, Stone Circle

This impressive 'flattened' circle, measuring about 88 m by 74 m in diameter, is in fact the fifth largest stone circle in Britain; there are now only eleven stones, of which only five are upright, but there were probably twelve originally.

42. TYNRON DOON
Fort NX 819939, sh 78, Tynron Doon, Fort

The summit of Tynron Doon has been fortified on several occasions, and small finds with a wide chronological range have been discovered. A stone wall forms the main defence, enclosing an area about 45 m by 40 m, and there is an impressive series of outer ramparts and ditches.

10. Stewartry

43. CASTLE HAVEN
Dun NX 593482, sh 83, Fort

Although it may seem unusual to find a small dry-stone fort or dun in this part of Scotland, several of the features of Castle Haven are not immediately comparable to those of the duns of southern Argyll, most particularly the presence of a concentric outer enclosure. The dun is D-shaped on plan with the chord of the D running along the cliff edge, the wall is of galleried construction, but its present height is due to extensive reconstruction in 1905.

44. MOTE OF MARK
Fort NX 845540, sh 84, Mote of Mark, Fort

Recent excavations have shown that the fortifications on the granite outcrop known as the Mote of Mark belong to about the middle of the first millennium AD; a timber-laced wall about 3 m thick encloses an area measuring about 80 m by 30 m. There was a timber gateway on the s side and a postern on the N. The conflagration of the fort has resulted in the destruction of the wall and the vitrifaction of the core material. The many interesting finds, including pottery, glass, and clay moulds, are now in the National Museum of Antiquities of Scotland, Edinburgh.

National Trust for Scotland: open at all times without charge.

45.   TRUSTY'S HILL
      Fort NX 589560, sh 83, Fort

This small timber-laced fort, situated 1 km w s w of Gatehouse of Fleet measures 27 m by 18 m internally; there are traces of a series of outworks, but the site is particularly interesting because of the presence of carvings related to Pictish symbol stones of N and E Scotland, belonging to around 700 AD. The most easily recognisable is the symbol known as the double-disc and z-rod. The symbols are to be found on a rock outcrop on the s E side of the fort near the entrance.

11. Wigtown

46.   BALCRAIG
      Cup-marked rocks NX 377443 and 373440,
      sh 83, Cup & Ring Marked Rocks

There are two fenced areas of cup-and-ring markings at Balcraig, the first in the field known as Far New England and the second in one known as Near Windlestraw. The former has two carvings of cup-markings with seven encircling rings; the other rock surface bears cups with eight, six and three encircling rings, some with radial grooves.

SDD: all times without charge.

47.   BARSALLOCH POINT
      Fort NX 347412, sh 82, Fort

Situated at the edge of a steep drop to the beach below, this fort is D-shaped on plan with the straight side along the cliff, and it encloses an area of about 0.1 hectare. Material from a single quarry ditch has been mounded up on either side to form a pair of ramparts. The ditch measures about 10 m across from crest to crest of the ramparts and about 3.5 m in depth; the entrance through the ramparts may still be detected on the N E.

SDD: all times without charge.

48.   CAIRNHOLY
      Chambered Cairns NX 517539 and 518540,
      sh 83, Chambered Cairns

The two chambered cairns of Cairnholy, excavated in 1949, are

important monuments to students of such tombs both because of their techniques of construction and because of the range of finds recovered; the objects from both sites are now in the National Museum of Antiquities of Scotland, Edinburgh.

The first cairn (43 m by 10 m) is not well preserved, but the chamber and the upright stones of the impressive façade make an imposing arrangement. It is likely that the simple chamber itself is the earliest part of the structure set perhaps within a small cairn, and that the outer part of the chamber and the façade belong to the second phase. After the final burials were placed in the tomb, the entrance was sealed and the forecourt area was filled with stones. The objects discovered included neolithic and beaker pottery and finely-made flint tools.

Situated some 150 m N, the second chamber is set within a smaller cairn which measures 21 m by 12 m. The chamber comprises two compartments, the innermost still retaining its roof, but the most impressive feature is the NW portal stone which still stands to a height of about 3 m. Again beaker pottery and flint objects were discovered.

sDD: all times without charge.

49.   DRUMTRODDAN
       Standing Stones and Cup-and-Ring Markings
       NX 364443 and 362447, sh 83, Standing Stones,
       Cup & Ring Marked Rocks

There is a setting of three stones, two standing and one now fallen, to the NE of the North Lodge of Monreith House. The erect stones, some 13 m apart, are both over 3 m in height and are set in a line running NE and SW; the fallen stone lies between them.

About 360 m to the N there are two outcrops of rock bearing cup-and-ring markings. Athough now suffering the results of weathering, cup-markings surrounded by up to five rings can still be seen; in some cases the individual motifs are joined by pecked channels.

sDD: all times without charge.

50.   FELL OF BARHULLION
       Fort NX 374418, sh 83, Earthwork

At the S end of the rocky ridge on the summit of the Fell of Barhullion there are the remains of a stone-walled fort defended by two walls. It measures some 40 m by 20 m internally, and the entrance is on the SW side where the inner wall measures about 3.4 m thick; the outer wall has been rather slighter.

< 48 (see also p.36)

51. KEMPS WALK
    Fort NW 975598, sh 82, Fort
This spectacular promontory fort is situated on Broadsea Bay, the internal area being some 90 m by 50 m. The complete perimeter of the promontory was originally, perhaps, encircled by a rampart with an outer work on all sides except the w. The steep flanks of the promontory would in themselves have provided considerable protection except on the N, where there is the only convenient access. The need for defence was greatest here, and the surviving remains are best preserved, namely three ramparts and ditches on the w side of the entrance and two on the E.

52. LAGGANGARN
    Standing Stones NX 222716, sh 76, Standing Stones
The two standing stones to the NE of the ruins of Laggangarn farm may possibly be prehistoric in origin, though they are now each decorated with a large incised cross, with smaller crosses in the angles formed by the arms and the shaft. Traditionally there were thirteen stones in the group at one time, but now only two survive.
    SDD: all times without charge.

53. MID GLENIRON
    Chambered Cairns NX 186610 and 187609, sh 82, Cairns
The excavations of two chambered cairns at Mid Gleniron between 1963 and 1966 were important because they showed that it was from a careful examination of the cairn material, quite apart from the cultural remains within the tombs, that a sequence of construction might be demonstrated.
    The first cairn is situated 300 m sw of Mid Gleniron farm on the N side of the farm road. In the first period the southernmost chamber was constructed within a small cairn; in the second period the simple N chamber was built also within an independent small cairn. Subsequently the lateral chamber was built and all three were incorporated within a larger mound with a crescentic façade which led into the northerly chamber of period two. The neolithic finds were not numerous, but the cairn had also been used as a burial place in Bronze Age times and seven cinerary urns containing cremation deposits had been inserted into the SE flank.
    The second chambered cairn, 120 m to the SE, is much ruined, but the stones of what is probably the original chamber are visible on the SE side. The present trapeze-shaped cairn belongs to the second phase of construction during which a

further chamber at the sw end was built, but this no longer survives.

The finds from the excavations are in Dumfries Museum.

54. RISPAIN
  Earthwork NX 429399, sh 83, Earthwork

This rectilinear earthwork, which is situated to the NW of Rispain farm, encloses an area measuring 68 m by 52 m. The deep v-shaped ditch has provided material for banks on either side of it, and excavation revealed the existence of a further outer ditch on the s and E sides, though this is not now visible. The gateway was found to be at the centre of the NE side. The shape of the earthwork is unusual, but radiocarbon dates suggest that it was constructed in the late Iron Age.

  SDD: all times without charge.

55. TORHOUSEKIE
  Stone Circle NX 382565, sh 83, Stones of Torhouse

This circle of boulders occupies what appears to be an artificial platform in an area known as the Machars; nineteen are set on what has been described as a flattened circle, some 21.5 m by 20 m overall, with an unusual arrangement of boulders at its centre where a stone is flanked by two more massive boulders.

There is an interesting setting of three stones, not in State guardianship, a little to the E.

  SDD: all times without charge.

56. THE WREN'S EGG, Port William
  Standing Stones NX 361419, sh 83, Stone Circle

A pair of standing stones have been set up a little to the E of a large glacial erratic. Although at one time it was suggested that these stones were all that survived of a pair of concentric circles, excavations in 1975 and a consideration of the topography indicate that this interpretation is unlikely. It is the massive erratic to which the name 'the Wren's Egg' has, with intentional humour, been applied.

  SDD: all times without charge.

FIFE

57. TORRY
Standing Stone NT 029865, sh 65, Standing Stone
This stone, situated beside an AA box, is 2.4 m in height and is
decorated with many cup-markings; the grooves are probably
natural in origin.

13. Kirkcaldy

58. BALBIRNIE
Stone Circle NO 285029, sh 59, not marked
This stone circle, excavated in advance of intended road development, has been re-sited within Balbirnie Park. The stone
circle (15 m by 14 m), a central setting of stones (the paving is
modern), and series of cists, including one with a decorated
side slab, are all visible. The range of pottery discovered during
the excavation (grooved ware, beaker, food vessel and cinerary
urn) shows that the site remained a focus for burials over a long
period of time.

Glenrothes Development Corporation: all times without
charge (guide leaflet available).

59. BALFARG
Henge Monument NO 281031, sh 59, not marked
The henge monument at Balfarg was excavated in advance of
housing development, but has now been landscaped and will
remain as an open area within the estate; the site offers one of
the best impressions both of the size of a henge monument and
of the scale of the task involved in digging out the ditches. A
series of timber and stone circles were discovered in the interior; the timber circle, now indicated by modern markers,
had a pair forming a 'porch' on the w side. Two concentric rings
of stone probably formed the next phase of construction, only
two uprights still survive, one forming a portal stone on the w
side of the entrance causeway into the interior. Grooved ware
pottery was found; a burial associated with an unusual
handled beaker was discovered near the centre (now marked
by a large slab).

Glenrothes Development Corporation: all times without
charge (guide leaflet available).

60. DUNEARN HILL
Fort NT 211872, sh 66, Fort
On the summit of Dunearn Hill are the extensive remains of

fortifications of two distinct periods; the earlier is that of an oval fort measuring 120 m by 40 m internally with an outer wall on the E affording additional protection to the entrance. At a later period a smaller circular fort was built in the interior; it measures about 36 m in diameter within a wall some 3.6 m in thickness. Several stretches of outer facing stones can still be seen.

14. North-East Fife

61. EASTER PITCORTHIE
Standing Stone NO 497039, sh 59, Standing Stone

This stone, situated about 550 m NW of the farmhouse, is a splendid monolith of red sandstone about 2.4 m high; the s face of the stone has been decorated with at least 33 cup-markings and two dumb-bell figures.

62. LUNDIN LINKS
Standing Stones NO 404027, sh 59, Standing Stones

These three standing stones are situated within a golf course, and intending visitors should check at the club-house that they will not disturb play; the stones may, however, be viewed conveniently from the edge of the course. They are up to 5.5 m in height and form the most impressive group of stones in Fife.

63. NORMAN'S LAW
Forts NO 305202, sh 59, Fort

The structures that occupy the summit of Norman's Law, to the N of the farm of Denmuir, illustrate a long period of fortification, even if the actual sequence of building is not altogether clear. The latest fortification is the best-preserved; it is an oval fort measuring some 50 m by 30 m within a wall about 3.6 m in thickness. There are two other walls, one enclosing the whole of the summit area (some 200 m by 75 m), and another forming an annexe on the sw side.

GRAMPIAN

There is a useful guide and gazetteer in *Early Grampian: a guide to the archaeology*, by Ian A.G. Shepherd and Ian B.M. Ralston (1979), Department of Physical Planning, Grampian Regional Council, Aberdeen.

15. City of Aberdeen

64. TULLOS HILL
    Cairns, sh 38, all indicated and named
On the ridge of Tullos Hill there are the remains of four cairns; the first, which is the least well preserved, is the Cat Cairn (NJ 951031), situated 500 m E of Nigg Church; the second, 800 m to the NE and known as the Baron's Cairn (NJ 957036), is 18 m in diameter and 1.5 m in height; Tullos Cairn, 500 m to the NNE (NJ 959041), is 20 m in diameter and 2.5 m in height; and the fourth, known as Crab's Cairn (NJ 963037) and situated 500 m to the E of Baron's Cairn, is some 14 m in diameter and 1.7 m high.

65. WEST CULTS
    Cairn NJ 883027, sh 38, Cairn
An impressive cairn measuring some 20 m in diameter and 5 m in height.

16. Banff and Buchan District

66. AIKEY BRAE
    Stone Circle NJ 958470, sh 30, indicated but not named
A notable recumbent stone circle; the uprights set on a broad stone bank measuring about 16.5 m by 13 m.

67. LONGMAN HILL
    Long Barrow NJ 737620, sh 29, Longman Cairn
This mound of earth, which is almost 70 m in length, probably covers a timber or stone ritual structure of early third millennium BC date; there is a heel-shaped mound at the NNE end, a round mound at the SSW end, linked by a barrow. 'Urns', probably secondary deposits, were found in the 1880s.

68. LOUDON WOOD
    Stone Circle NJ 960497, sh 30, Stone Circle
The four surviving stones of this recumbent stone circle are situated in a forest 4 km WNW of Mintlaw; only the recumbent and the W flanker are still upright, but the bank in which the stones were set is still comparatively well preserved.

69. MEMSIE
    Cairn NJ 976620, sh 30, Cairn
This huge cairn of stones (24 m in diameter and 4.4 m high),
one of the best-preserved Bronze Age burial mounds in Scotland, tellingly illustrates the work effort involved in the construction of many prehistoric funerary monuments in Scotland. Formerly there were another two cairns nearby.
    SDD: all times without charge.

69

70. 'ST MARNAN'S CHAIR', Marnach Church
    Standing Stone NJ 597502, sh 29, church indicated
Within the churchyard there is a particularly impressive
standing stone (2.5 m high), perhaps originally one of the
flanking stones of a recumbent stone circle; the smaller stone
to the N is not thought to be in its original position.

17. Gordon

71. BALQUAIN
    Stone Circle NJ 735240, sh 38, Stone Circle
This recumbent stone circle, standing in a field to the NE of
Mains of Balquain farm, is notable for its tall outlying pillar of
white quartz (a reminder of the importance of the magical
properties that may have been attributed to such stones in
prehistoric times), for the well-massed group of stones form-

ing the recumbent and its flankers, and for the groups of cup-markings on several of the upright stones.

72. BARMKIN OF ECHT
Fort NJ 726071, sh 38, Fort

The summit of the hill is defended by a series of ramparts and walls representing several periods of fortification, which are well illustrated on the air photograph; three ramparts and ditches form the outermost defence with two ruined walls set within. The triple ramparts are pierced by five entrances, but the presumably later stone walls employ only two.

72

73. CULLERLIE
Stone Circle NJ 785042, sh 38, Stone Circle

A well-preserved circle of eight standing stones about 10 m in diameter, within which eight kerb-cairns have been built; excavation has revealed traces of burning, perhaps of a ritual nature, on the original land surface and in a pit at the centre of the circle.

SDD: all times without charge.

74. EASTER AQUHORTHIES
Stone Circle NJ 732207, sh 38, Stone Circle

An impressive recumbent stone circle about 20 m in diameter, with a massive recumbent stone almost 4 m long and eleven uprights; the recumbent has a pair of supporting slabs set at right angles to it projecting to the inside of the circle.

s D D : all times without charge. (See frontispiece.)

75.   LOANHEAD OF DAVIOT
      Stone Circle and Enclosed Cremation Cemetery
      NJ 747288, sh 38, Stone Circle

This recumbent stone circle and adjacent cremation cemetery form an important ritual complex of later third and second millennium BC date. The monoliths are set on the diameter of a circle of 19.5 m diameter, but the recumbent itself and the flanking stones are well inside this line. The upright stones are surrounded by small stone 'cairns', and excavation revealed deposits of cremated bone. The interior of the circle is covered by the low cairn, which is clearly visible on the photograph; this covered a layer of burning with further indications of burials.

The adjacent cremation cemetery was enclosed within two arcs of ditch and with lines of stones; the burials were placed in grave-pits inside cinerary urns. At the centre of the site were the cremated remains of a body below what was interpreted as the pyre.

s D D : all times without charge.

75

76. MIDMAR
Stone Circle NJ 699064, sh 38, Stone Circle

Within the churchyard at Midmar is a recumbent stone circle about 17 m in diameter; the recumbent and its flanking stones form a well-massed group.

77. MITHER TAP O'BENNACHIE
Fort NJ 682224, sh 38, Fort, also indicating access path

A mass of tumbled stone survives to show that the fort on the summit of the Mither Tap must originally have been very splendid; the magnificent situation, however, still makes this an impressive site to visit.

78. OLD KEIG
Stone Circle NJ 596193, sh 37, Stone Circle

Although this circle is in a rather sorry state of preservation, the recumbent stone is a magnificent block, weighing about 50 tons.

79. SUNHONEY
Stone Circle NJ 715056, sh 38, Stone Circle

An impressive circle of twelve stones 26.7 m in diameter stands in trees 200 m NW of the farm; the recumbent group is notable both for the size of the main stone and for the group of cup-markings on its surface.

80. TAP O' NOTH
Fort NJ 484293, sh 37, Fort

Although the approach to this fort is not to be undertaken lightly, the Iron Age work on the summit of Tap O' Noth (563 m OD) is testimony to the determination of its builders. Considerable quantities of wood would have been required to bond the rubble wall together, and when this was fired, either accidentally or in the course of attack, the timber and core fused to form a vitrified mass; the fort measures about 100 m by 30 m internally.

81. WORMY HILLOCK, Finglenny
Henge Monument NJ 449307, sh 37, not marked

This tiny but well-preserved henge monument is situated in the forest of Clashindarroch. It consists of an annular bank with internal ditch enclosing a central platform some 6 m in diameter; there is an entrance causeway through the bank and ditch on the SE.

18. Kincardine and Deeside

82. CULSH
Souterrain NJ 504054, sh 37, not marked

This souterrain is an excellently preserved example of its class, and still extends underground for a distance of 14.3 m; intending visitors will need a torch to examine the building techniques of the walls and the flat roofing slabs. Excavations for example at Newmill, Perth and Kinross, have shown that souterrains might have been integral parts of upstanding timber houses rather than being isolated structures; they were probably stores.

SDD: all times without charge.

83. GARROL WOOD
Stone Circle NO 723912, sh 38, Stone Circle

This recumbent stone circle, also known as 'The Nine Stanes', is situated in a clearing in a forestry plantation, about 100 m walk from the minor road between Blairydryne and Strachan, on the E side of the forest track. Excavations in 1904 revealed a complex relationship between the upright stones and the central ring-cairn which butts the recumbent. At the centre of the ring-cairn there was a funnel-shaped pit which contained a deposit of cremated bone. The surrounding 'circle' is largely intact and measures some 18 m by 14.5 m.

There are two other stone circles within fields to the N and NW at West Mulloch (NO 722921) and Elsie (NO 717915) respectively; the former comprises six stones, including the recumbent, surrounding a cairn some 16 m in diameter, the latter has eight uprights besides the recumbent with its flanking stones, and forms a circle about 25 m in diameter around a central ring-cairn.

84. GOURDON
Long Cairn NO 818706, sh 45, Long Cairn

This cairn, probably concealing a neolithic mortuary structure, is about 45 m long and stands to a height of almost 2 m.

85. TOMNAVERIE
Stone Circle NJ 486034, sh 37, Stone Circle

A recumbent stone circle some 17 m in diameter; several of the stones have now fallen, but the recumbent is an impressive slab, 3.3 m long. The surrounding view is extensive, but the present situation at the edge of a quarry is unfortunate.

SDD: all times without charge.

19. Moray

86. AUCHINDOWN CASTLE
NJ 348374, sh 28, Auchindown Castle

The castle, which has a complex building history beginning in the 15th century during the reign of James III, is set within the remains of a prehistoric fort.

SDD: the Castle is not open to the public, but the surrounding earthworks are open at all times without charge.

87. AUCHORACHAN
Standing Stone NJ 209278, sh 36, Standing Stone

A tall stone, 1.7 m in height; tradition has it that it was once moved by a farmer, but was then replaced as he was 'troubled' by his action.

88. DOUNE OF RELUGAS
Fort NJ 003495, sh 27, Fort

A small fort, measuring some 50 m by 30 m internally, with several large lumps of vitrified material still visible near the entrance on the E. An outer work bars access to the fort on the N and W flanks, but on the other two the steep drop to the River Divie may have been thought to provide adequate protection.

89. LITTLE CONVAL
Fort NJ 294393, sh 28, Fort

An interesting unfinished fortification at a height of 550 m OD, four defensive lines seem to have been envisaged and these are indicated by marker trenches.

90. 'SCULPTORS CAVE', Covesea
Caves NJ 175707, sh 28, Caves

This cave was occupied on at least two separate occasions, first in the Late Bronze Age and later in the Iron Age; incised on the walls at the entrance are several Pictish symbols and thus a third period of occupation may be envisaged. The cave has been excavated on two occasions (1927 and 1979); the finds from the earlier work are in the National Museum of Antiquities of Scotland.

91. 'THE DEIL'S STANES', Innesmill
Stone Circle NJ 289640, sh 28, Stone Circle

A stone circle with an unusually large diameter (33.5 m), of which five stones remain upright, the tallest being at least 1.8 m high. The two fallen stones are not in their original positions.

HIGHLAND

92. ACHKINLOCH, Loch Stemster
    Standing Stones ND 188418, sh 12, Standing Stones

This unusual U-shaped setting of stones, situated close to the road at the SW end of Loch Stemster, originally comprised more than fifty stones set at right angles to the outline of the figure; over twenty stones are now missing. The shape and layout of this site appears to be unique in Scotland.

93. CAMSTER
    Chambered Cairns ND 260442 and 260440,
    sh 12, Grey Cairns of Camster

The long cairn at Camster has an important role in our understanding of the multi-period nature of the construction of chambered tombs; although it was known that the position of the NE chamber in relation to the long mound was unusual, as there was a bend in the passage, the precise relationship of the various features was not known until recent excavations. Now it is clear that this simple chamber was originally set within a small cairn with a dry-stone wall over 1 m in height forming its perimeter. The chamber at the centre of the long cairn was perhaps originally bounded by a small circular cairn, but both small cairns were subsequently contained within a magnificent long cairn with a monumental horned façade formed by dry-stone walling at its NE end. This has been sensitively restored following the recent excavations. The cairn is about 60 m in overall length and 20 m in breadth across the horns. Access to both chambers was made possible after the construction of the long cairn by the elongation of the passage of the NE chamber on a rather different axis from the original passage and by the lengthening of the passage of the central tomb.

The round cairn, situated about 200 m SE, measures about 18 m in diameter and 3.6 m in height. The dry-stone walling at the entrance, which is on the ESE, has been restored; the entrance passage is low (only 0.75 m high in places) and access is on hands and knees for about 6 m. Four upright stones on either side of the passage help to support the roof. The chamber is divided into three main compartments by upright slabs, roofed both by lintels, and by the use of corbelling to a height of 3 m. Pottery and flint was found in the course of excavation; the pottery is now lost.

SDD: all times without charge.

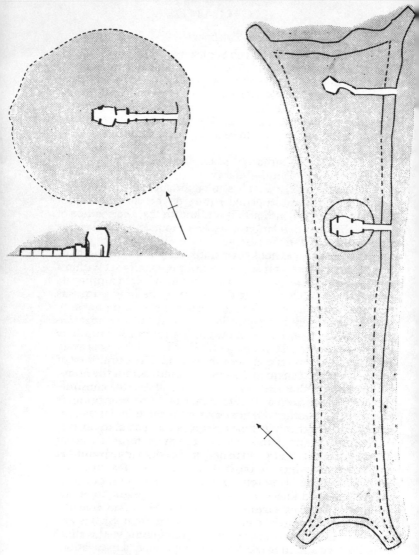

*Camster Round Cairn, plan and elevation;
Camster Long Cairn, plan*

93 round

94. CNOC FREICEADAIN
Chambered Cairns ND 013654 and 012653,
sh 12, Chambered Cairns

The first cairn, which measures over 67 m by 16 m, probably represents several periods of construction, including perhaps an independent round cairn at its s w end with the addition of a long cairn, with distinct 'horns' at its NE end. Several upright slabs attest to the presence of a number of chambers, but in the absence of excavation, the history of the site can be a matter only of speculation.

Situated 120 m s of this mound, on the actual summit of Cnoc Freiceadain is the long mound known as Na Tri Shean; it is probably, but not certainly, chambered, and its long axis lies at right angles to the other cairn. Measuring at least 75 m in length, it has the appearance of two heel-shaped, and horned, cairns set back to back with a rather lower mound joining the two presumably independent features; the NW end stands 2 m, and the SE end 3 m in height.

SDD: Cnoc Freiceadain only, all times without charge.

95. GARRYWHIN, Cairn of Get
Chambered Cairn ND 313411, sh 12, Cairns

This little passage-grave is set within a cairn with two pairs of projecting 'horns'; the entrance is on the sw where there are two portal stones at the centre of a horned façade and the other pair of 'horns' are on the opposing NE end of the cairn. The short passage leads to a rectangular outer compartment and a circular chamber. Excavation in 1886 uncovered a thick deposit of cremated and unburnt bones in the central chamber, along with leaf-shaped arrowheads, flint and sherds of pottery. In the outer compartment there were seven or eight inhumation burials with the skulls all placed to the right side of the entrance.

SDD: all times without charge.

96. GARRYWHIN
Stone Rows ND 314413, sh 12, not marked

This setting of small upright stones radiating from a small cairn is an example of an unusual class of site. The cairn, which is about 10 m in diameter, covered a cist containing the remains of an inhumation burial, associated with what was probably a beaker or a food vessel. The six rows of uprights, erected at intervals of between 2.5 m to 3 m, fan out from the cairn towards the sw.

97. HILL O' MANY STANES, Mid Clyth
Stone Rows ND 295384, sh 11, Stone Rows

This remarkable series of stone rows consisted originally of over 250 uprights set in twenty-two rows, aligned approximately N and s in a fan-shaped arrangement diverging to the s. None of the stones is tall, the largest being under 1 m in height, but the construction of the rows has been very consistent and accurate.

SDD: all times without charge.

98. WAG OF FORSE
Dun and Settlement ND 204352,
sh 11, Dun & Settlement

This complex settlement and defensive site excavated in 1939 and 1946 has several building phases, but the relationship between them is not altogether clear. The name 'wag' may derive from the Gaelic word 'uamh', which means cave. One of the earliest buildings is a circular structure about 14 m in diameter with a dry-stone wall about 1.2 m thick. The entrance is still visible on the NNE side where the wall has been deliberately thickened; there is a guard cell on one side and a stair, which allows access to the top of the wall, on the other.

Around the dun there are later structures the date of which is uncertain, but they bear a close resemblance to buildings outside several of the Caithness brochs. Finds from the site included saddle querns (see photo below), a fragment of a rotary quern, part of a lignite ring and sherds of pottery.

22. Inverness

99.   BALNUARAN OF CLAVA

Chambered Cairns NH 757444, sh 27, Chambered Cairns
The three major monuments of Balnuaran of Clava form an awe-inspiring memorial to the religious beliefs and architectural abilities of early man.

The sw cairn is a passage-grave with a surrounding stone circle; the circle is some 32 m in diameter with the passage on the sw side of the cairn leading to a central chamber about 4 m in diameter. There are several cup-marked stones: on the se side of the passage a stone bears several possible cup-markings; a boulder on the w side of the chamber just at the entrance bears twelve cup-markings; and a stone of the outer ring on the w side also has a number of cup-markings on its inner face. When the chamber was excavated about 1828 two fragmentary vessels and a quantity of cremated bone were recovered.

The central tomb of the group is a ring-cairn with nine stones of the surrounding circle surviving, three of which are joined to the cairn by causeways, rather like the spokes of a wheel. A scatter of cremated bone was found within the central chamber.

A little to the w of this cairn and beneath the trees that form the w perimeter of the site there is a small kerb-cairn some 3.6 m in diameter; this was found to contain a grave-pit for an inhumation burial associated with quartz pebbles. One of the kerb-stones is decorated with cup-markings.

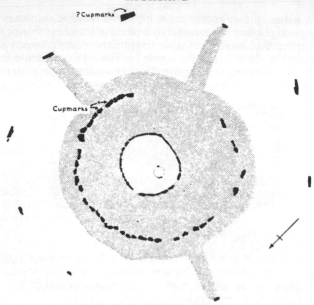

Balnuaran of Clava, Central

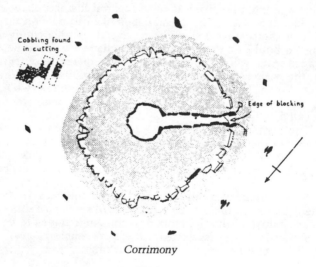

Corrimony

The cairn known as Balnuaran of Clava North-East is another passage-grave surrounded by a circle of standing stones; two cup-marked stones are incorporated into its fabric, one as a kerb-stone of the cairn on the N side and the other at the inner end of the NW side of the passage. The kerb-stone is particularly interesting with cup-markings, a cup-and-ring marking as well as a series of pecked channels.

SDD: all times without charge.

100. CORRIMONY

Chambered Cairn NH 383303, sh 26, Chambered Cairn
This is an attractive passage-grave in the Clava tradition situated at the W end of Glen Urquhart some 30 km WSW of Inverness. The cairn is surrounded by a ring of upright standing stones 21.3 m in diameter and measures about 15 m by 14 m in diameter. The long passage leads to a central circular chamber some 3.6 m in diameter, which was once completely corbelled and still stands to a height of about 2 m. Excavation revealed the stain of a crouched inhumation burial accompanied by a burnt bone pin. The massive flat stone on the cairn, weighing about two tons and decorated with many cup-markings, may originally have been the final roofing slab of the chamber.

SDD: all times without charge.

100

101. CRAIG PHADRIG
     Fort NH 640452, sh 26, Fort

The fort, which is within a Forestry Commission plantation, is still clear of trees and offers views over the Black Isle. Two vitrified walls enclose an area measuring 75 m by 23 m, the inner wall being particularly massive and still stands to a height of 1.2 m internally. The fort was built in the fourth century BC, but there is also evidence of occupation during the Dark Age.

23. Lochaber

102. CAMAS NAN GAELL, Ardnamurchan
     Chambered Cairn NM 560619,
     sh 47, Cladh Chiarain marked

Only a portion of the chamber of this cairn of the *Clyde* group survives, as well as one horn of the façade. The setting of the tomb within the small enclosed bay gives an excellent impression of the habitat of the earliest agriculturalists, combining access to the sea, the easily tilled soils at the head of the bay, and the rich hunting grounds of the hillsides beyond.

Some 90 m S of the cairn there is a small burial ground marked as Cladh Chiarain and just to the SW of it there is a tall stone, perhaps originally a prehistoric standing stone; it is now decorated with two crosses and what may be a dog.

103. DUN GRUGAIG, Gleann Beag
     Broch NG 851158, sh 33, Dun Grugaig

This semi-broch, which is situated some 2 km SE of the better preserved Dun Troddan and Dun Telve, occupies the summit of a craggy rock to the E of the Abhainn a Ghlinne Bhig. D-shaped in plan, it measures 14.3 m by 11.5 m within a stout wall some 4.3 m in thickness. Although the site has not been excavated, a scarcement ledge and cells within the thickness of the wall can still be seen, as well as an entrance passage with such characteristic broch features as door checks and a bar-hole.

Visitors to this site will pass the small passage-grave of Balvraid (NG 845166); the passage-grave is set within a square cairn, now much robbed, but excavation in 1965 uncovered sherds of neolithic and beaker pottery, lignite beads and flint implements.

104. DUN TELVE and DUN TRODDAN
     Brochs NG 829172 and 833172, sh 33, Broch; Broch

These two brochs provide excellent demonstrations of all the

104 *Dun Telve*

main features of broch construction, and, perhaps because both are built on a solid base, their walls still stand to heights of 10 m and over 7.6 m respectively. Dun Telve is on the valley floor and measures 9.8 m in diameter within a wall some 4 m in thickness. The outer face has a distinct batter, but the inner is vertical with traces of two scarcement ledges, doubtless to provide support for an upper storey and a timber roof.

The central court of Dun Troddan measures 8.5 m in diameter and the wall some 4 m in thickness; excavations about 1920 revealed a ring of post-holes in the interior, and these probably supported timber buildings or an upper gallery.

SDD: all times without charge.

105. GREADAL FHINN, Ardnamurchan

Chambered Cairn NM 476639, sh 47, Chambered Cairn
Although the cairn itself is not well preserved (now measuring some 22 m in diameter and no more than 0.6 m in height) the upright stones forming a small passage-grave of Hebridean type are virtually intact, as well as a small, and rather more central, chamber or cist. Whether this is primary to the cairn or a later insertion, only excavation will tell. The view from the site, however, is magnificent.

26. Skye and Lochalsh

106. DUN ARDTRECK, Skye

Broch NG 334358, sh 32, Dun Ardtreck
This semi-broch occupies a superb position at the edge of sheer cliffs dropping to the sea below; it is D-shaped on plan, and the galleried wall encloses an area measuring about 13 m by 10 m. The monumental entrance, made all the more impressive by having a raised threshold, has had the customary door-checks with a bar-hole (and presumably slot) to keep a stout timber door in position.

107. DUN BEAG, Struanmore, Skye

Broch NG 339386, sh 32, Dun Beag, Broch
This well-preserved broch measures about 11 m in diameter within walls up to 4.3 m in thickness. The entrance has checks to support a wooden door; several features can still be seen within the thickness of the wall including a small bee-hive cell, and a chamber with a stair of about twenty steps. On the NW there is an extensive mural gallery, the sill of its entrance door-way raised about 0.6 m above the level of the interior of the broch.

108. DUN GRUGAIG, Elgol, Skye
Dun NG 535122, sh 32, Dun Grugaig

On the E side of the Strathaird peninsula this dun stands on a narrow promontory some 15 m above the sea. The wall, which encloses an area about 15 m by 7 m, is thickest on the NW side, where there is access across a narrow neck of land, but elsewhere it is thinner, and now more ruinous. The entrance is well-preserved, displaying not only its door-jambs, bar-hole and slot, but also several of the roofing lintels of the passage. The massive nature of the wall at this point, where it stands to a height of 4 m, has allowed traces of a gallery over the entrance to survive; it may be that the series of steps on the inner face of the dun wall to the E of the entrance was originally designed to allow access to this higher gallery.

109. DUN HALLIN, Hallin, Skye
Broch NG 256592, sh 23, Dun Hallin, Broch

The broch, situated 700 m NE of Hallin, is worth visiting not only because of its excellent preservation but also for the extensive views over Loch Dunvegan and Loch Snizort; it measures 11 m in diameter within a wall up to 3.4 m thick, and the entrance is on the SE where there are the remains of flanking guard-cells or chambers. Within the tumbled wall debris on the SW the remains of a mural gallery can still be seen.

Additional defence has been provided by an outer wall, which encloses an area measuring about 46 m by 38 m.

110. DUN FIADGAIRT, Dunvegan, Skye
Broch NG 231504, sh 23, Dun Fiadhairt, Broch

This splendid broch occupies the summit of a rocky outcrop 2 km NW of Dunvegan Castle; it was excavated in 1914 and as a result both the inner and outer face have been partly cleared of fallen masonry. Measuring 9.5 m in diameter within a wall some 3.6 m in thickness, the broch was originally entered from the W where the passage is flanked by guard-cells. On the N side of the interior, short passages provide access to two cells within the thickness of the wall, the eastern one containing a staircase. Opposite the entrance there is a second passage, though the outer end of this is now blocked; midway along its S wall there is the doorway into a narrow gallery that runs within the thickness of the broch wall for most of its S circuit.

111. DUN RINGILL, Kilmarie, Skye
Dun NG 561170, sh 32, Dun Ringill

Situated on a rocky promontory on the W side of Loch Slapin, there is an interesting dun defended on all sides except the E by a massive wall up to 4.5 m in thickness; the central area measures about 22 m by 17.5 m and contains a secondary rectangular building, and there is also some secondary building at the inside of the entrance. The entrance, which is on the NW, retains its door-jambs, bar-hole and slot. Within the thickness of the dun wall on the s side there is a narrow gallery leading to a cell measuring about 5.5 m by 1.5 m with its walls still standing to a height of about 4 m.

Situated in trees 900 m WNW of Dun Ringill there is an oval cairn, known as Cnocan nan Gobhar, measuring 22 m by 17.5 m and up to 4.5 m in height (NG 552173). In 1926 a short cist containing a cremation deposit accompanied by a beaker was found near the top of the mound, but it is not known what other structures may be hidden by the cairn material.

112. RUBH' AN DUNAIN, Skye
      Chambered Cairn NG 393163, sh 32, Chambered Cairn
At the end of the peninsula on the s side of Loch Brittle, there is a well-preserved passage-grave within a circular cairn about 20 m in diameter and 3.4 m in height. Several uprights of the forecourt remain with a stretch of dry-stone walling between. The lintelled passage leads to a circular chamber about 2.2 m in diameter and still standing to a height of over 2 m. Excavation in 1931 and 1932 revealed several burials associated with neolithic and beaker pottery; the finds are now in the National Museum of Antiquities of Scotland.

There is an interesting little promontory fort 400 m to the SE on the further side of Loch na h-Airdhe (NG 395159); the cave marked on the map at NG 399162 has produced beaker pottery, and evidence of later iron smelting.

27. Sutherland

113. DUN DORNADILLA
      Broch NC 457450, sh 9, Dun Dornaigil
The height to which this broch survives and the large triangular stone over the entrance passage are perhaps its most remarkable features. It measures 8.2 m in diameter within a wall some 4.2 m thick and up to 6.7 m high on the NE; the interior is filled with tumbled masonry, but the entrance to a chamber within the thickness of the wall is still visible.

SDD: all times without charge.

114. EMBO
      Chambered Cairn NH 817926, sh 21, not marked
This cairn has been consolidated following excavation and

stands within a car-park; it is oval, measuring 12.8 m by 9 m, and contains two passage-graves and two cists. The s chamber measures 2.3 m by 1.7 m, with a short entrance passage 1.5 m long, and is constructed of six upright slabs with dry-stone walling between. The chamber contained several inhumations and sherds of beaker ware. A secondary cist has been inserted into the chamber; within it there was an inhumation burial, a food vessel and sixteen beads of jet. The n passage grave was more ruined, but it was found to contain remains of an inhumation burial. A further cist had been set into the cairn material just to the s of the n passage-grave; it contained the burials of two infants accompanied by a food vessel and fragments of a beaker. At least nine secondary cremation deposits were found within the cairn, one of which had been inserted into the n chamber. One of the most remarkable features of the excavation was the discovery of a great range of animal, fish and bird bones in various contexts in the chambers and in the cairn, including squirrel, guillemot, and Ballan wrasse, providing an unusual insight into the ritual practices of neolithic and bronze age people.

LOTHIAN

28. East Lothian

115. BLACK CASTLE
Fort NT 580662, sh 67, Fort

This well-preserved circular fort is a good example of the medium-sized forts of se Scotland; it measures about 110 m in diameter within twin ramparts with a central quarry ditch. There are two entrances, one on the w and the other on the s.

116. CHESTERS, Drem
Fort NT 507782, sh 66, Fort

This fort is more remarkable for its position, overlooked as it is from the adjacent ridge, than for the preservation of the remains. The innermost rampart encloses an area of 115 m by 45 m and outside it there is a complex series of outer ramparts, especially around the entrances on the NW and E. Within the interior there are several foundations, some perhaps of prehistoric date but others of comparatively modern origin.

SDD: all times without charge.

117. EASTER BROOMHOUSE
Standing Stone NT 680766, sh 67, Standing Stone

This tall stone, over 3 m in height, situated in the middle of a field to the s of Easter Broomhouse farm, bears three cup-markings on its w face.

118. KIDLAW
Fort NT 512642, sh 66, Fort

This spectacular fort has three ramparts with external ditches enclosing an area about 110 m in diameter; there are entrances both to the E and W, and within the interior there are traces of a concentric palisade trench, besides three later homesteads.

119. KINGSIDE HILL
Stone Circle NT 626650, sh 67, not marked

This small stone circle, which is situated on the NW slope of Kingside Hill about 350 m N of the public road, comprises thirty stones and has a diameter of 12 m; the stones are small and protrude at most 0.4 m above ground level. At the centre of the site there is a larger stone (though still only 0.6 m by 0.5 m and 0.2 m in height) set in a low cairn surrounding it.

120. LOTH STONE
Standing Stone NT 578741, sh 67, Standing Stone

This stone is situated about 300 m s s w of the foot of Traprain Law, and is said to indicate the grave of the mythical king Loth, after whom the Lothians are named; it has been moved 47.5 m s of its original position, but nothing was found in the course of the excavation of the stone.

121. TRAPRAIN LAW
Fort NT 581746, sh 67, Fort

This hog-backed ridge, standing to a height of 100 m, is one of the landmarks of the East Lothian plain; excavations and chance finds show that it has been a focus of prehistoric activity since neolithic and bronze age times, although the visible structural remains largely date from the iron age; their sequence and date are not easy to interpret. The large number of finds from the site, including the magnificent hoard of late Roman silver found in 1919, are on display in the National Museum of Antiquities of Scotland, Edinburgh.

The two most visible lines of defence are probably the latest in the sequence, the final phase being represented by a wall some 3.6 m in thickness running along the flank of the ridge on the N and enclosing a broad terrace on the W. This wall encloses an area about 12 ha (30 acres), and a date between the

<116 (above), 126

third and fifth centuries AD is usually suggested for its construction.

The earlier fort, perhaps the tribal capital of the *Votadini*, enclosed an area of 16 ha, its rampart taking in a number of hut-platforms on the lower slopes of the N flank of the hill.

29. City of Edinburgh

122. CAIYSTANE
Standing Stone NT 242683, sh 66, not marked

This shapely stone now stands on the E side of Caiystane View, on the N side of Oxgangs Road; it measures about 3 m in height and is decorated on its E face with a number of cup-markings quite close to the ground.

National Trust for Scotland: all times without charge.

123. CRAIGIE HILL
Fort NT 153758, sh 65, Fort

On the summit of the ridge known as Craigie Hill, there are traces of two distinct periods of defence; the earlier is represented by a series of three walls running along the w flank to enclose an area measuring about 230 m by 45 m, and the later by an oval stone-walled fort at its N end. Within the interior of the earlier fort, the platforms of several houses may be seen, depending on the state of the vegetation.

124. HOLYROOD PARK
Forts, sh 66

The remains in Holyrood Park are not easy to interpret, but their accessibility and position give them a particular interest. On Salisbury Crags (NT 270732) a long wall cuts off the nose of the plateau, but whether it is all of prehistoric date is perhaps more open to question. Round the main massif of Arthur's Seat (NT 278729), Dunsapie (NT 282731), and above Samson's Ribs (NT 274725) there are also the remains of defences, in the last two cases certainly of prehistoric date. It is likely that these forts indicate one of the centres of power of the *Votadini*.

SDD: the sites fall within the Royal Park of Holyrood.

125. NEWBRIDGE
Barrow and Standing Stones NT 123726, sh 65, Tumulus

This mound is about 30 m in diameter by 3 m high, and, although partly excavated in the last century, it is likely that the primary burial deposits remain intact. Around the barrow, but not in fact concentric to it there are three upright stones the tallest of which is over 2 m in height. A fourth upright, 320 m to the E, may be an outlying stone to this group.

30. Midlothian

126. BRAIDWOOD
Settlement NT 193596, sh 66, Settlement

This complex settlement occupies a low hill which overlooks Eight Mile Burn from the N. The most prominent feature is an earthwork, comprising two ditches with a medial bank, but within the interior there are traces of a concentric palisade trench enclosing an area measuring 54 m by 36 m. Within the earthwork at least twelve timber houses are visible; two appear to be earlier than the palisade trench, but some of the others are later.

127. CASTLELAW, Glencorse
Fort and Souterrain NT 229638,
sh 66, Fort and Souterrain

This fort is situated on the summit of a rounded knoll immediately NW of Castlelaw Farm and is defended by three ramparts and ditches enclosing an area about 82 m by 37 m; within the inner ditch on the E side, a souterrain with a bee-hive chamber had been constructed. Although excavated on two occasions, the sequence of building of the fort is not altogether clear, and the middle rampart is now the most noticeable feature. There is an entrance at the centre of all sides except the N, and excavation of the E gate in 1948 revealed a timber-lined passage some 3 m in width.

The souterrain is a remarkable structure over 20 m long and up to 2 m in both width and height; there was no sign of roofing lintels nor of the quantity of stone that might have been expected from a corbelled roof, and it is likely that the original roof was at least partly of timber. Midway along the passage on the W side there is an entrance into a bee-hive chamber 3.4 m in diameter and about 2 m in height. The small number of finds included a fragment of a Roman bowl, glass and iron as well as a bronze buckle of approximately second century AD date.

SDD: standard opening hours (apply to key keeper at Crosshouse Farm, Milton Bridge), (guide leaflet available).

128. CRICHTON
Souterrain NT 400619, sh 66, Souterrain

This souterrain, situated 1.5 km E of Crichton Church in the centre of an arable field, is remarkable for the number of dressed blocks of Roman masonry used in its construction. The gallery is 15 m long and varies between 1.6 m and 2 m in width; the roof lintels are original, one with a carving sometimes described as a Pegasus, but the arched roof is modern. A torch is essential to see the method of construction and with a cross light to pick up the diamond broaching of the Roman stones.

31. West Lothian

129. CAIRNPAPPLE HILL
  Henge Monument and Cairn NS 987717,
  sh 65, Cairnpapple Hill

The important site on the summit of Cairnpapple Hill commands extensive views in all directions, particularly to the N. The sequence of activity on the site uncovered by excavation in 1947–8 is a key one for an understanding of later neolithic and Bronze Age monuments in SE Scotland. The first period consisted of an arc of seven small pits, six of which contained deposits of cremated bones, two accompanied by bone skewer pins; at the centre of the arc there were sockets for three upright stones. In the second period, the henge monument was constructed with opposing entrances through the bank and ditch. Within there was an oval setting of upright stones and to the W of the centre, a grave pit with an inhumation burial, two beaker vessels and wooden objects. Beside one of the stones on the E side of the circle there was a further crouched inhumation accompanied by another beaker. During the third period the circle was dismantled and a cairn was built to protect a cist burial with a food vessel, and this also covered the earlier stone setting round the central beaker grave. A concrete cover has been built to indicate the profile of this cairn and visitors may descend into the interior, into what would originally have been solid cairn material, to view the grave settings. In the fourth period the cairn was enlarged to enclose two cremation burials in inverted cinerary urns. Finally four unaccompanied inhumation burials were interred within the E part of the site.

  SDD: April to September standard opening hours, but closed on Thursday afternoon and on Fridays; October to March closed.

ORKNEY

The nineteen prehistoric monuments of Orkney held in trust by the Secretary of State for Scotland and cared for by the Scottish Development Department are described in a comprehensive guide-book, *The Ancient Monuments of Orkney*, by Anna and Graham Ritchie (1978), HMSO. The monuments provide perhaps the best overall impression of the life of early man in northern parts of Scotland. The chambered cairns belong to two main groups – the first, the Orkney-Cromarty-Hebridean group, and the second named after the tomb of Maes Howe. The former possess chambers, often rectangular, divided into compartments by large upright slabs; Blackhammer, Knowe of Yarso, Midhowe, Taversoe Tuick and Unstan. The tombs of the Maes Howe class have a passage leading to a central chamber off which there are several cells: Cuween Hill, Holm of Papa Westray, Wideford Hill are the other examples of this class in State care. The settlement sites of Knap of Howar and Skara Brae provide vivid insights into the domestic architecture of neolithic Orkney in the first half of the third millennium BC, the former is associated with a style of pottery found in the Orkney-Cromarty-Hebridean tombs, and the latter with grooved ware, which is also found in tombs of Maes Howe type and within the stone circle at the Stones of Stenness.

Although most of the finds from major Orcadian prehistoric sites are in the National Museum of Antiquities of Scotland, Edinburgh, the archaeological collection in Tankerness House Museum in Kirkwall includes material from Skara Brae and the broch of Gurness, and there are often special exhibitions of finds from current excavations.

130. BLACKHAMMER, Rousay
    Chambered Cairn HY 415276, sh 6, Chambered Cairn
This chambered cairn was excavated in 1936 and is now protected by a concrete cover which is entered through a hatch on the s side; measuring 22 m by 8.2 m overall, the cairn has a rectangular central chamber divided by upright flagstones into seven compartments. The original entrance passage is in the middle of the s side. Two inhumation burials were found in the course of the excavation, one in the entrance passage and the other in the compartment at the w end.
    SDD: all times without charge.

143

131. BURRIAN, North Ronaldsay
      Broch HY 762513, sh 5, Broch & Settlement
This broch is situated close to the shore on the s tip of the
island and is now threatened by coastal erosion. Its walls,
however, still stand to a height of 3 m and the entrance-
passage, which opens immediately on to the rocks of the fore-
shore, is still visible. The landward side of the site is protected
by four lines of ramparts, but these are not easy to detect on the
ground. The site was excavated in 1870 and the remarkable
series of small finds recovered (now in the National Museum
of Antiquities of Scotland) illustrate the Iron Age, and Pictish
occupations of the site; they include pins, combs, pottery,
spindle whorls, gaming pieces and an early Christian incised
cross-slab with an ogam inscription.

132. CASTLE OF BURWICK, South Ronaldsay
      Fort ND 435843, sh 7, Fort & Settlement
The excellent natural defences of this precipitous promontory
have been augmented by three banks and ditches which cut
across the narrow neck of land at the only point of access.
Hollows in the surface of the interior represent the ruined
foundations of houses.

133. CUWEEN HILL, Mainland
      Chambered Cairn HY 364128, sh 6, Chambered Cairn
This tomb occupies a superb position on the NE side of Cuween Hill; set within a mound some 16 m in diameter, the
chamber is entered by a low passage on the E side. The central
chamber is rectangular, its walls standing to a height of 2.3 m,
and there is a small cell on each side, that on the w side being
divided into two. Eight inhumation burials were discovered
when the chamber was excavated, with five skulls on the floor
of the central chamber; within the same context were found
the skulls of twenty-four dogs.
   SDD: all reasonable times without charge.

134. DWARFIE STANE, Hoy
      Chambered Tomb HY 243004, sh 6, The Dwarfie Stane
This spectacular block of red sandstone is sited on the E side of
the valley between Quoys and Rackwick, about 4 km from the
landing place at Mo Ness. The stone, which measures 8.5 m by
4.5 m and is 2 m in height, has a rock cut passage on the w side
giving access to twin cells. There is a blocking stone in front of
the entrance. The tomb is now thought to be a variety of the
sort of tomb represented by Taversoe Tuick on Rousay.
   SDD: all times without charge.

135

135. GRAIN
Souterrain HY 442116, sh 6, Souterrain

This souterrain was originally discovered in 1827, though it was not excavated until 1857; the passage is some 4.7 m long giving access to an oval chamber. The roofs of both the passage and the chamber are covered by flat slabs, with four pillars providing additional support in the chamber.

SDD: all reasonable times without charge (apply to key keeper).

136. GURNESS, Mainland   ∧ 136>
      Broch HY 382268, sh 6, Broch of Gurness
The broch on the promontory known as Aikerness was excavated in several seasons from 1929 and is remarkable because
of both the preservation of the buildings and the range of small
finds recovered, examples of which are displayed in the site
museum. Around the broch there are three additional ramparts
with quarry ditches, and the main entrance, like that of the
broch itself, is on the E. The broch has for the most part a solid
base, but there are guard-cells and short galleries on either side
of the entrance. Between the broch and the innermost ditch
there is a bewildering collection of houses, many with well-
preserved hearths. One of the latest houses has been rebuilt
close to the site museum; it consisted of a series of cells round
a central area and was entered from the w. This type of house
has recently been identified as Pictish, and there is a rough
design for a Pictish stone on display in the site museum. A
Viking grave has also been discovered at Gurness; a woman
buried in a stone-lined pit was accompanied by oval bronze
brooches, a necklet, an iron sickle and an iron knife; these
objects are in Tankerness House Museum, Kirkwall.
    SDD: standard opening hours (guide leaflet available).

137. HOLLAND, North Ronaldsay
      Standing Stone HY 752529, sh 5, Standing Stone
This spectacular stone stands to a height of over 4 m and is
perforated by a small hole about half way up. There is a tradition that the islanders used to gather round the stone at New
Year and dance in the moon light.

138. HOLM OF PAPA WESTRAY
      Chambered Cairns HY 509518, sh 5, Chambered Cairn
There are two chambered tombs, and a possible but unexca-
vated third tomb, on this tiny uninhabited island. The best
preserved is an extraordinary chamber of Maes Howe type,
which possesses fourteen side-cells; there are a number of
decorated stones in its wall, of which the best is the lintel
above the entrance to the SE cell, ornamented with hollows
and 'eye-brow' motifs. The other stalled cairn is situated at the
N end of the island.
      SDD: all reasonable times without charge (apply to key
keeper at Holland, Papa Westray).

138

139. KNAP OF HOWAR, Papa Westray
      Settlement HY 483518, sh 5, Knap of Howar
The little neolithic settlement site known as Knap of Howar,
the excavation of which was completed in 1975, comprises
two houses built side by side. The larger, which is also the
earlier house, measures about 9.7 m by 4.8 m internally within
walls of dry-stone construction about 1.5 m in thickness; the
interior is divided into two by a partition of upright stones and
by two timber posts, which no doubt also helped to support the
roof. A massive saddle quern remains in position in the rear of
the house. The second house, with an entrance on the seaward

side and a short passage leading directly from the first house, is rather smaller (8 m by 3 m) but it has several cupboards or storage compartments built into the walls. The main surviving feature is a central hearth. Radiocarbon dates show that the houses were occupied between about 3500 BC and 3100 BC; the pottery found shows that the site was in use by people who buried their dead in tombs such as Unstan. The excavation also demonstrated the economy of the inhabitants of Knap of Howar, with stock-breeding, collecting shell-fish and hunting wild animals.

SDD: all times without charge.

140. KNOWE OF YARSO, Rousay
Chambered Cairn HY 405280, sh 6, Chambered Cairn

This cairn, which measures about 15 m by 8 m and up to 1.8 m in height, contains a rectangular central chamber subdivided by upright slabs into a series of compartments. Excavations in 1934 revealed unusually well-preserved burials, at least 29 individuals being represented; 15 skulls were found in a line at the bottom of the wall of the innermost compartment with their faces turned towards the wall. Flint and bone objects, sherds of beaker and food vessel wares, and animal bones were also recovered; a radiocarbon date indicates that the tomb was in use around 2900 BC.

SDD: all times without charge.

141. KNOWES OF TROTTY, Mainland
Barrows HY 342174, sh 6, Tumuli

The barrow cemetery to the s of the farm of Netherhouse is best known for the rich grave goods which accompanied a burial in the largest of the group. This mound, which lies 120 m s of the farm, is about 18 m in diameter and over 3 m high, and was partly excavated in 1858 when a cist containing cremated bones was discovered; on a flat stone in a corner of the cist there were four discs of thin gold foil together with amber beads and space-plates, which were probably cut down from elaborate amber necklaces. The finds are now in the National Museum of Antiquities of Scotland, Edinburgh.

142. MAES HOWE, Mainland
Chambered Cairn HY 318128, sh 6, Maeshowe

This tomb is rightly considered to be one of the most splendid achievements of early prehistoric Europe, for it displays a very high standard of architectural skill as well as a most sensitive use of stone as a building material. The chamber is covered by a mound of clay, peat and stones, which measures

35 m in diameter by over 7 m in height, and is set on a platform encircled by a low bank and ditch. Radiocarbon analysis of peat from the ditch suggests that the tomb was built sometime before 2700 BC. A passage some 9 m long leads from the outer door-checks to the main chamber with its three side-cells.

The main chamber is about 4.5 m square and survives to a height of almost 4 m; the upper part of the corbelled roof is modern reconstruction. Tall pillars face the stone buttresses in each corner, providing essential support for the roof, and even where the walls begin to converge inwards towards the roof the naturally oblique face of the slabs has been used to advantage in maintaining a smooth wall-face.

The entrances to the side-cells are above floor-level, and the massive stones with which they were presumably once blocked, lie on the floor of the main chamber. No gravegoods or burials were found, but the presence on the walls of the main chamber of 24 runic inscriptions and drawings of a dragon, a walrus and a serpent knot bear witness to Norse intrusions in the 12th century AD.

SDD: standard opening hours, but closed on Saturday and Sunday (guide leaflet available). Only twelve people are admitted to the monument at one time.

143. MIDHOWE, Rousay
       Broch HY 371308, sh 6, Brochs

The spectacular coastal situation on the shores of Eynhallow Sound, with views across to the promontory of Aikerness, provides an added incentive to visit the well-preserved broch of Midhowe. The broch has a gallery at ground level, though this has been partly filled in prehistoric times to avoid collapse; it has been defended on the landward side by two ditches with a substantial wall in between. The interior of the broch is divided into two by large upright stones with hearths and cubicles on both sides. The remains of further buildings, including one with a smelting hearth, remain on the N side of the broch.

The small finds from the excavations, now in the National Museum of Antiquities of Scotland, include simple objects of bone and stone as well as more sophisticated objects of bronze including ring-headed pins and brooches.

There is another mound, probably the tumbled remains of a broch a little to the NW, but this has not been excavated and is not in the guardianship of the State.

SDD: all times without charge.   142 >

144. MIDHOWE, Rousay
        Chambered Cairn HY 372306, sh 6, Chambered Cairn
A very large and well-preserved tomb comprising a stalled
chamber over 23 m long set within an oblong cairn; the outer
wall-face of the cairn is remarkable for the arrangement of the
stone slabs in a herringbone pattern, which is best seen on the E
side. The chamber is divided into twelve compartments, several of which are furnished with low stone benches, on or under
which burials were placed.
        SDD: all times without charge.

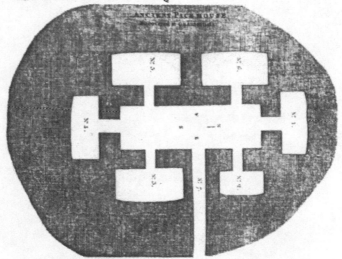

'Ancient Pickhouse discovered at Quanterness'

145. QUANTERNESS, Mainland
        Chambered Cairn HY 418120, sh 6, Chambered Cairn
This magnificent chambered tomb, with six side chambers off
a main chamber, was constructed probably before 3000 BC. It
lies on the N slope of Wideford Hill, and the covering cairn is
approximately 30 m in diameter. Quanterness was first described by the Rev. George Barry, in 1805, and the plan of the
chamber, in his *History of the Orkney Islands*, is the earliest
known publication of a Scottish passage grave. Re-excavated
in the early 1970s, it is not at present open to the public, but a
'reconstruction' of the cairn is given on p.40 by courtesy of
Colin Renfrew.

143

146. QUOYNESS, Sanday
Chambered Cairn HY 677377,
sh 5, Quoyness Chambered Cairn

A circular mound set on a low platform encloses a most spectacular tomb of Maes Howe type, similar to the recently excavated, but inaccessible, tomb at Quanterness on mainland
Orkney. The walls of the main chamber soar to a height of
almost 4 m, and there are six side-cells.

SDD: all reasonable times without charge (apply to key
keeper).

147. RENNIBISTER, Mainland
Souterrain HY 397126, sh 6, Souterrain

An excellent example of the Orcadian type of souterrain, in
which a narrow passage leads from ground-level down into an
oval underground chamber; the chamber is furnished with
small alcoves in the wall and with upright pillars to help to
support the roof.

SDD: all reasonable times without charge (apply to key
keeper).

148. RING OF BRODGAR, Mainland
Henge Monument and Stone Circle, and Barrows
HY 294134, sh 6, Ring of Brogar; Cairns

The Ring of Brodgar is perhaps the most awe-inspiring site in
Scotland, both because of its situation on a promontory between two lochs and because of the completeness of the stone-
circle and surrounding ditch. Originally there was a circle of
sixty stones set within the rock cut ditch which probably once
had an outer bank, though the evidence for this is at best
inconclusive. Recent excavations have shown that the ditch
was up to 3 m in depth and 9 m across, with two opposing
entrance causeways, one on the NW and the other to the SE. Of
the thirty-six stones that survive, the only authentic decoration is the series of Norse tree-runes (undeciphered) on a
broken stump virtually due N from the centre of the site. The
interior, which measures about 113 m in diameter, has not
been excavated.

There are several small mounds to the SE of the circle which
are presumably of Bronze Age date, as well as two larger barrows, including Salt Knowe situated about 100 m SW. To the E
of the site is the upright known as the Comet Stone; this is set
on a low platform and originally formed a setting with at least
two other stones, the stumps of which can still be seen. Finally
the visitor should examine the mounds on the E side of the

road, the more northerly of which, Plumcake Barrow, contained two cists with cremation burials; it is not clear how
much of the more southerly is indeed artificial.

sDD: all times without charge.

149. SKARA BRAE, Mainland
      Settlement HY 231188, sh 6, Skara Brae
The neolithic settlement of Skara Brae, occupied between
about 3100 BC and 2450 BC, was preserved beneath blown sand
until it was partly exposed in 1850; in 1924 the site was placed
under the guardianship of the State. Excavation and consolid-
ation from 1927, with additional work in 1972 and 1973 to
recover environmental evidence, have provided an unusually
full picture of the structural sequence and of the day-to-day life
of the inhabitants, described in detailed guide books about the
site and the recent excavations. There appear to be two main
house types: the first is built round a central hearth with bed
recesses within the wall, the second, and later, type also has a
central hearth but the beds are brought into an enlarged floor
area. The most evocative features of the domestic life of the
neolithic inhabitants are, perhaps, the stone-built dressers,
designed to receive flat-based storage vessels. As well as providing the radiocarbon dates on which the chronology of the
site depends, the recent excavations have shown that the inhabitants were fishermen as well as farmers. Cattle were the
most important domesticated animal, with fewer sheep or
goats, and small numbers of pigs. Hunting of wild animals also
played a part, perhaps seasonally, in the economic life of the
community.

sDD: standard opening hours (guide book and interim report
on recent excavations available).

150. STANE OF QUOYBUNE, Birsay, Mainland
      Standing Stone HY 253262, sh 6, Standing Stone
This is an impressive stone, almost 4 m high, with an affec-
tionate place in local folklore: on New Year's Day morning it
is said to go down to the nearby loch for a drink.

151. STONES OF STENNESS, Mainland
      Henge Monument and Stone Circle HY 307125,
      sh 6, Stones of Stenness
Three impressive uprights remain of what was once a circle of
twelve occupying the interior of a henge about 30 m in diameter within a rock-cut ditch and the slight remains of an
external bank. There was a single entrance causeway on the N
side. The crooked stone on the N side of the circle was found

and re-erected in 1906 and its appearance may not be quite original. Excavations in 1973 revealed a central setting of stones, no longer visible, with cremated bone, charcoal and grooved ware pottery, and similar ware was found at the w terminal of the rock and ditch. This style of pottery and radiocarbon dates in the early third millennium BC suggest that it was used by the same sort of community as that living at Skara Brae.

There were once two outlying stones to the N – the Watch Stone, and the Stone of Odin, but only the former survives at a point 170 m to the NNW. The Stone of Odin, felled amidst local consternation in 1814, was perforated by a small hole, and tradition has it that bargains were sealed and love plighted formally by grasping hands through the hole.

Another outlying stone, not always accessible, is the Barnhouse Stone some 700 m to the SE of the Stenness ring.

SDD: all times without charge.

152. TAVERSOE TUICK, Rousay
      Chambered Cairn HY 426276, sh 6, Chambered Cairn
This is an unusual double tomb, in which two stalled chambers have been built one on top of the other, each with its own entrance passage through the circular covering mound. In addition, a miniature tomb only 1.5 m long was built at the edge of the platform on which the mound stands. Finds from all three chambers and passages include Unstan ware bowls, 35 shale disc beads and a broken stone macehead.

SDD: all times without charge.

153. UNSTAN, Mainland
      Chambered Cairn and Fort HY 283118,
      sh 6, Chambered Cairn
A fine example of a stalled burial chamber within a circular mound; there is also a side-cell opening off the main chamber. Gravegoods included a large number of sherds from Unstan ware bowls, four leaf-shaped arrowheads and a flint implement. Remains of inhumation burials were found in each compartment and there were two crouched inhumations in the side cell.

The tip of the promontory to the N of the tomb is cut off by two low banks and ditches, but the date of this little fortification is unknown.

SDD: standard opening hours (apply to key keeper at Unstan).

< 149

154. WIDEFORD HILL, Mainland
    Chambered Cairn HY 409121, sh 6, Chambered Cairn
A rectangular chamber of Maes Howe type with three side-cells; it is enclosed within a circular mound in which two inner rings of strengthening walling have been exposed by excavation.
    SDD: all times without charge.

SHETLAND

The displays in the museum in Lerwick illustrate the material equipment of prehistoric as well as later times in Shetland. There is a particularly fine collection of neolithic polished stone axes and of the porphyry knives which are found only in Shetland. The bulk of the finds from Jarlshof and Clickhimin is in the National Museum of Antiquities of Scotland, Edinburgh. There is a helpful guide – *A Guide to Prehistoric Shetland*, by Noel Fojut (1981), Shetland Times, Lerwick.

155. BROCH OF BURLAND, Dunrossness, Mainland
    Broch HU 445360, sh 4, Broch of Burland
This is a spectacular example of a broch with massive outer defences, but it is also a very dangerous site and unsuitable for visitors with children. The small promontory on which the broch stands is bordered by precipitous cliffs, and the landward approach is barred by a close-set series of three ditches alternating with three great stone-faced ramparts. The broch, now perilously close to the edge of the cliff, survives to a height of about 3 m.

156. CLICKHIMIN, Lerwick, Mainland
    Fort and broch HU 464408, sh 4, Broch
A remarkable sequence of prehistoric buildings may be seen on a small island in a loch on the outskirts of modern Lerwick. Reached by a causeway, the site spans almost a thousand years of human occupation, from the stone-built houses of the mid first millennium BC through several stages of fortification to a wheelhouse settlement in the mid first millennium AD. The stone wall of the fort encloses a massive blockhouse inside the entrance, but the interior is now dominated by the remains of the later broch, probably built in the first century AD. The broch itself was later modified by the insertion of a domestic wheelhouse.
    SDD: all times without charge (guide-book available).

156>

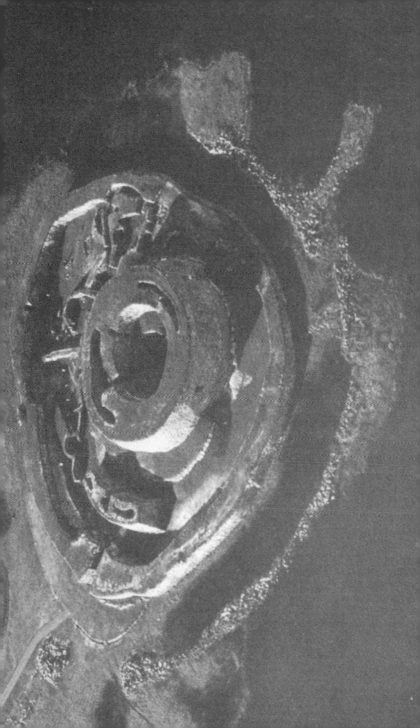

157. THE GIANT'S STONES, Hamnavoe,
     Northmavine, Mainland
     Standing Stones HU 243805, sh 3, The Giant's Stones
Set about 20 m apart in rough moorland just to the E of Hamnavoe, there are two standing stones about 2 m high.

158. ISLESBURGH, Northmavine, Mainland
     Chambered Cairn HU 334684, sh 3, Chambered Cairn
Most of the chambered cairns in Shetland belong to a special
class which is unique to Shetland, although they are related to
tombs elsewhere; this type is characterised by a heel-shaped
cairn of stones covering a rectangular or trefoil-shaped burial
chamber, and most are small when compared with tombs
elsewhere. Some, like Islesburgh, appear to be related to contemporary domestic settlements and fields. Set on a low promontory a little to the W of Mavis Grind, the typical heel-
shaped outline to the cairn is clearly visible here, with the
entrance to the rectangular burial chamber set in the centre of
the slightly concave façade.

159. JARLSHOF, Dunrossness, Mainland
     Broch and Viking-age Settlement HU 398095,
     sh 4, Jarlshof
Jarlshof is justly famous for its archaeological complexity and
for the name bestowed on it by Sir Walter Scott. Inexplicably,
this particular spot on the eastern shore of the west Voe of
Sumburgh has been selected repeatedly for settlement from
around 2000 BC until the laird's house called Jarlshof in *The
Pirate* was built about AD 1600. The visible buildings include
domestic houses of the first millennium BC, a broch now
partially destroyed by the sea, exceptionally fine wheelhouses,
an extensive Viking-age settlement, a medieval farmstead and
the laird's house.
     SDD: standard opening hours, but closed on Tuesday and on
Wednesday afternoon (guide book available).

160. THE LANDBERG, South Haven, Fair Isle
     Fort HZ 222722, sh 4, Fort
Perched on a steep and narrow promontory, this fort overlooks
the twin landing-places of South Haven and North Haven on
the NE coast of Fair Isle. The fort-builders took advantage of a
natural rift across the promontory, deepening it and creating a
stone-faced rampart behind it; in front of the rift there is a
series of low banks and ditches, three to the E and two to the W
of the entrance causeway. The rectangular house-foundation
visible inside the fort is probably of later date.

161. MOUSA, Dunrossness, Mousa
    Broch HU 457236, sh 4, Broch of Mousa

The sound between the small island of Mousa and the mainland of Shetland was once dominated by two broch-towers, one on Mousa itself and the other on the high promontory of Burraland. The broch of Mousa is still a spectacular and brooding presence, its wall unbroken save for the doorway and rising to a height of 13.3 m. It may always have been an extreme example of its class, for it seems unlikely that many other brochs were built so high, but it does convey a memorable impression of the militaristic society that created it. Within the broch wall there are three cells at ground level and a stairway leading up through six mural galleries to the top of the wall as it survives.

SDD: standard opening hours (apply to key keeper; guide book available).

161   *Mousa, by George Low, 1774*

161

162. NESS OF BURGI, Dunrossness, Mainland
Fort and Blockhouse HU 388085, sh 4, Fort

This remarkable fort lies on the Scatness peninsula, which forms the w side of the great bay known as the West Voe of Sumburgh, at the very tip of the mainland of Shetland. A small promontory on the E side of the main peninsula has been cut off by a substantial stone-faced rampart with a ditch on either side. An entrance through the rampart leads to a massive stone-built blockhouse, more than 22 m long (the s end is incomplete) and about 6 m wide; this has been restored, but it had survived to a height of about 2 m with several lintel-slabs still in position over the passages. The building is divided into two by an entrance passage in which there are door-checks and bar-holes to allow a portable door to be set and barred into position. A low passage off one side of the main passage and another opening from the fort interior lead into guard-cells within the blockhouse.

SDD: all times without charge.

163. PUNDS WATER, Northmavine, Mainland
    Chambered Cairn HU 324712, sh 3, Chambered Cairn
This tomb is set in a conspicuous position on a small knoll in moorland, some 3 km NW of Mavis Grind. Large stones forming the kerb of the cairn are visible, and the trefoil-shaped burial chamber is well preserved, its wall still intact to a height of about 1.4 m.

164. STANYDALE, Walls, Mainland
    'Temple', and House HU 285502 and HU 288503,
    sh 3, Settlement and Field System
The first is a massive structure clearly related in its overall heel-shaped outline to burial cairns, but its size suggests that it had a different function, perhaps that of a meeting-place or a temple. It has walls up to 4 m thick, and the enclosed oval chamber is almost 12 m long and up to 9 m wide. Projecting picrs create small compartments in the larger (W) end of the house, and two large axial post-holes once held substantial timber uprights to support the central ridge of the roof.

There are several houses in the vicinity of the great 'temple', of which the excavated example at HU 288503 is typical of early domestic structures in Shetland. It is oval with thick stone walls and contains one large, roughly oval room with two cupboards or recesses in the wall and a small round cell opening off the far end of the room. The entrance is sheltered by an outer extension of the main house wall.

Within 4 km from Stanydale there are several similar settlements, field-systems and burnt mounds, including those on Ness of Gruting (HU 277484 and 281483), Scord of Brouster (HU 255516) and Pinhoulland (HU 259508), although not all of these are well-preserved.

SDD: all times without charge.

165. VAASETTER, Fair Isle
    Burnt Mound HZ 207715, sh 4, Burnt Mound
This is one of the largest burnt mounds in Shetland, measuring about 37 m by 27 m and surviving to a height of about 3 m. No fewer than nine such mounds survive on this island as testimony to a flourishing community in late prehistoric times.

166. VEMENTRY
Chambered Cairn HU 295609, sh 3, Chambered Cairn
The small island of Vementry, off the W coast of mainland
Shetland, is dominated by the hill of Muckle Ward, and on the
summit is one of the finest and best-preserved chambered
tombs in Shetland, surely a prestigious place to be buried. The
cairn proper is circular, but it is set on a large heel-shaped
platform with a façade carefully built of large blocks of stone.
The burial chamber is trefoil-shaped with a long entrance
passage, and the lintels over the NE cell are still in position.

STRATHCLYDE

32. Argyll and Bute

167. ACHNABRECK, Mid Argyll
Cup-and-Ring marked Rock NR 855906,
sh 55, Cup-&-Ring marked Rocks
On the hillside overlooking the Crinan Canal and Achnabreck
farm there is a spectacular area of cup-and-ring markings on
the edge of a forest; the complex designs include 135 cup-and-
ring markings, some with as many as seven rings, and also
double spirals. The area covered by the carvings and their
complexity is without parallel in Scotland. Another exceptional group of cup-and-ring markings occurs on a smaller
exposure of rock about 140 m to the E (the approach through
the forest can be muddy).
SDD: all times without charge.

168. ACHNACREE and ACHNACREEBEAG, Lorn
Chambered Cairns NM 922363 and 929363, sh 47,
Chambered Cairn; Burial Chambers (wrongly sited)
These two chambered cairns stand at the N edge of the Moss of
Achnacree, the former in trees just to the s of the minor road
that forms the N extremity of the Moss, and the latter some
300 m w of the farm of Achnacreebeag on the E side of the
Abhainn Achnacree.
Carn Ban, Achnacree is a very large cairn over 24 m in
diameter by up to 4 m in height and though in 1871 a complex
passage grave was discovered, the only part of the chamber still
visible is a capstone in the hollow at the top of the cairn.
In contrast, little of the cairn material of the Achnacreebeag
tomb survives but the two burial chambers are virtually intact.

Excavations in 1968–70 showed that the NW chamber was probably the earlier and that the passage grave on the SE side of the cairn had been added at a later date. The earlier chamber is a simple dolmen-like structure of five upright boulders and a capstone. The passage-grave has ten uprights with dry-stone walling between them; the capstones are no longer in their original positions.

The finds from both sites are in the National Museum of Antiquities of Scotland, Edinburgh.

169. ARDNACROSS, Mull
  Cairns and Standing Stones NM 542491,
  sh 48, Standing Stone

Occupying a terrace on the hillside to the WSW of Ardnacross farm there is an interesting group of three small cairns, with low boulder kerbs set between two parallel lines of stones, only one of which is still upright. The site was clearly an important local burial place, perhaps in the second half of the second millennium BC. There is another kerb-cairn to the NNW of the farm at NM 545496; the denuded remains of a broch, of which the entrance passage and stretches of the wall face can still be detected, are situated over 600 m NNE of the farm at NM 550499.

170. BALLOCHROY, Kintyre
  Cist and Standing Stones NR 730523,
  sh 62, Standing Stones

An interesting setting of three standing stones in a line running NE and SW and a massively-constructed burial cist, which was formerly covered by a large cairn. It has been suggested that the stones form a prehistoric observatory with the central stone aligned towards the mountain of Corra Beinn on Jura recording midsummer sunset about 1800 BC.

171. BALLYGOWAN, Mid Argyll
  Cup-and-Ring marked Rock NR 816977,
  sh 55, Cup-&-Ring marked Rock

A rock sheet with as many as sixty cup-markings and eleven cup-and-ring markings, five of which are surrounded by three rings.

  SDD: all times without charge.

172. BALUACHRAIG, Mid Argyll
  Cup-and-Ring marked Rock NR 831969,
  sh 55, not marked

An extensive outcrop decorated with both cup-and-ring markings and plain cup-markings; there are twenty-three cup-and-ring markings, of which some fifteen have two rings, and over 130 cup-markings. To the N there is a smaller sheet of rock with six cup-markings.

s DD : all times without charge.

172

173. BALLYMEANOCH, Mid Argyll
Henge Monument and Standing Stones, NR 833962 and 833964, sh 55, Henge and Standing Stones
Access to this complex of sites is not normally possible, but

166

the two linear settings of standing stones can be seen from the road; several of the stones are decorated with cup-and-ring markings. The remains of a henge are just visible 150 m to the ssw.

174. BORGADEL WATER, Kintyre
Dun NR 625061, sh 68, Dun

This well-preserved dun occupies an isolated knoll which offers superb views across the North Channel at the s tip of the Mull of Kintyre; it measures about 13 m in diameter within a wall up to 4 m thick and 2 m high and the entrance, which is checked for a door, is on the w.

175. CAIRNBAAN, Mid Argyll
Cup-and-Rink marked rocks NR 838910, sh 55, Cup-&-Ring marked Rocks

There are two interesting sheets of cup-and-ring markings on the hillside above the Cairnbaan Motor Inn.

sdd: all times without charge.

176. CARRADALE POINT, Kintyre
Fort NR 815364, sh 68, Fort

This fort, which occupies the summit of Carradale Point, is cut off from the mainland at high tide. Measuring about 56 m by 23 m internally, the fort wall was originally strengthened by timbers, the burning of which has caused the vitrification of the core. Substantial masses of vitrified material are visible, particularly on the e side. A number of short stretches of walling block gullies leading up to the summit.

177. CORRIECHREVIE, Kintyre
Cairn NR 738540, sh 62, Cairn

A large burial cairn measuring about 28 m in diameter and 5 m in height is situated 200 m NW of Corriechrevie farm.

178 DERVAIG, Mull
Standing Stones, sh 47, Standing Stones; Standing Stones; not marked

There are three separate alignments of standing stones to the NE, E and SE of the village of Dervaig, two of which include impressive upright stones. The most remote group, in a clearing in a forest on Maol Mor (NM 435351), comprises three upright and one fallen stone; the second situated in a small clearing on the N side of the road between Dervaig and Tobermory (NM 439520) is of five stones, though only two are still upright; and the third to the s of the road about 850 m ESE of Dervaig, is of three stones (NM 438516), now none higher than 1.1 m.

179. DUNADD, Mid Argyll
   Fort NR 837935, sh 55, Dunadd

Although the surviving fortifications on this prominent rock massif are of Dark Age date, the impressive series of defences cutting off various terraces may help to evoke the type of citadel in use in earlier times. The main access has been through a rocky defile, once defended by stout wooden gates. In the interior there would originally have been houses of timber and stone. Carvings on the rock surface just below the summit include a rock cut basin, a foot-print, a boar and an ogam inscription. The fort was probably one of the main strongholds of the *Scotti*, who moved into Argyll from N Ireland before about AD 500, and the basin and the foot-print have sometimes been interpreted as forming part of the inauguration ceremonies of the kings of the *Scotti*.

   SDD: all times without charge.

179

180. DUN AISGAIN, Mull
   Dun NM 377452, sh 48, Dun Aisgain

This dun is situated in a spectacular position 600 m SW of Burg on a rocky knoll overlooking the interesting deserted settlement of Burg. Both the inner and outer wall-faces are unusually well preserved, the wall enclosing a circular central area some 10.5 m in diameter. Other features of note are the entrance on the W, the intra-mural gallery on the NE and the encircling outwork.

181. DUNCHRAIGAIG, Mid Argyll
      Cairn NR 833968, sh 55, Cairns

A massive cairn, over 30 m in diameter and 2 m in height, excavated on at least three occasions, but it is unlikely that the primary burial has been disturbed. On the SE side there is an unusual boulder-walled burial chamber, covered by a very large capstone (4.3 m by 2.5 m), which contained burials both by cremation and inhumation. At the centre of the cairn a smaller cist, which contained a cremation burial accompanied by a food vessel, is still visible. A third cist, which had similar contents, can no longer be seen.

SDD: all times without charge.

182. DUN MOR VAUL, Tiree
      Broch NM 042492, sh 46, Broch

Along with Clickhimin and Jarlshof in Shetland this broch is probably the most extensively studied of its class; excavations between 1962 and 1964 have elucidated several phases of construction and reconstruction, and, although not preserved in a manner that befits its importance, the site is an exciting one to visit.

It is situated some 300 m NW of the township of Vaul, and is surrounded by a massive irregular outwork. In all, the broch wall is 4.5 m in thickness and encloses an area 9.2 m in diameter, but there is a well-preserved gallery at ground level, in contrast to that at Tirefour on Lismore. The complex entrance is on the E side, with the door-jambs, bar-hole and guard cells still clearly visible. The broch was probably built about the middle of the first century BC, but the excavations showed that the site had been occupied both earlier and perhaps more importantly later in the early centuries AD when it became the focus for an undefended farming community.

183. DUN NA MUIRGHEIDH, Mull
      Fort NM 412236, sh 48, Fort

This fort occupies a promontory which is protected by sheer rock-faces on all sides except the S, where there are no less than four walls. The innermost, which extends down the E and W flanks of the promontory, reaches a maximum thickness of 5.2 m on the S, adjacent to a complex entrance, and the interior measures about 30 m by 20 m. The later, possibly medieval, buildings within and to the SE of the fort are themselves of some interest.

184. DUN SKEIG, Kintyre
      Fort and Duns NR 757571, sh 62, Fort; Dun

The series of fortifications on the summit of Dun Skeig over-look the entrance to West Loch Tarbert from a height of about 140 m above sea level – a position best appreciated from the deck of an Islay steamer. Traces of the first period of fortifica-tion are slight, but a wall enclosed the complete summit of the hill. The second period is represented by a dun (26 m by 18 m internally) at the s end of the summit, the wall of which is completely vitrified. In the third period a smaller dun (15 m by 13 m) was built at the N end; its wall, which incorporates pieces of vitrified stone robbed from the earlier dun, is well preserved and the entrance is clearly visible on the NE.

185. ETTRICK BAY, Bute
    Stone Circle NS 044667, sh 63, Stone Circle
This attractive stone circle is situated in a ring of trees at the centre of a field at the head of Ettrick Bay.

186. GLEBE CAIRN, Mid Argyll
    Cairn NR 833989, sh 55, Cairn
This cairn is massive, measuring 33.5 m in diameter and about 4 m in height. Nothing is visible of the cists containing food vessels, in one case accompanied by a necklace of jet beads, which were revealed by excavation in 1864.
    SDD: all times without charge.

187. GLENVOIDEAN, Bute
    Chambered Cairn NR 997705, sh 62, not marked
This well-preserved chambered cairn is situated 450 m SE of Kirkmichael farm; the main chamber is at the N end with lateral chambers on the E and W sides; several stretches of the wall forming the E perimeter of the cairn are still visible. Excavated between 1963 and 1971 the site is an important one for the demonstration of the multi-period nature of such tombs. The axial chamber set within a round cairn forms the first phase; and the lateral chambers covered by additional cairn material, the second; the formation of the trapezoidal cairn enclosing the three main chambers is the third. There are then further phases of activity including the insertion of a cist burial with a cremation on the E side and a corn-drying kiln which was entered from the W. The pottery and flintwork recovered from the excavation are in the Bute Museum, Rothesay.

188. KILDONAN, Kintyre
    Dun NR 780277, sh 68, Dun
An easily accessible dun on the seaward side of the road from Campbeltown to Carradale; it is D-shaped in plan measuring

19 m by 13 m internally. The construction of the wall in two thicknesses contributes to its stability. The entrance, on the sw side has door-checks and bar-holes; other features of interest include a double mural stair to provide access to the wall head on the w and a small intramural cell on the NE.

189. KILMICHAEL GLASSARY, Mid Argyll
   Cup-marked rock NR 863945, sh 55, not marked
Situated on a steeply sloping rock surface to the w of Kilmichael Glassary Church, there are groups of well-executed rock carvings including both single cup-marks and more complex figures.

   SDD: all times without charge.

190. KINTRAW, Mid Argyll
   Standing Stone and Cairns NM 830050,
   sh 55, Standing Stone; Cairns
A site no longer examined for its own magnificent position overlooking Loch Craignish, but because of its position in the pantheon of archaeoastronomical observatories, Kintraw now presents a sad appearance to the visitor. The splendid standing stone, some 4 m in height, has fallen and has been re-erected. The large cairn, 14.5 m in diameter, has been excavated, but has been restored in such a way that none of the interesting features, including projecting portal stones on the sw quadrant, can be seen. The smaller kerbed cairn to the w of the standing stone can barely be discerned.

   There is considerable doubt about whether the 'platform' in the hillside is indeed a prehistoric feature, and its part in the interpretation of the site as an observatory for the mid-winter solstice is thus a subject for discussion. Perhaps for these reasons alone the site is worthy of careful examination.

191. LECCAMORE, Luing
   Dun NM 750107, sh 55, Dun
This site shows many of the classic features of the class of small stone-walled forts known as 'duns'. It makes the best use of its defensive position on the summit of a rocky ridge and measures about 20 m by 13 m within a dry-stone wall up to 5 m in thickness. There are, unusually, two entrances, and that at the sw end has well preserved door-jambs with a bar-hole and slot to secure a stout wooden door. The NE entrance has a small guard-cell on the w side with a stair that has allowed access to the wall-head. The dun has been further defended by an outer wall and by rock-cut ditches.

192. LOCHBUIE, Mull
    Stone Circle NM 617251, sh 49, Stone Circle
At the head of Loch Buie, and within the policies of Lochbuie
House there are several well preserved monuments including
standing stones and a small cairn (NM 614252), the latter
disfigured by a transverse excavation trench. The stone circle,
situated to the N of the house, comprises eight original stones,
with one modern marker, the tallest being 1.75 m in height and
situated in the SW quadrant. There are two outlying standing
stones, that on the SW side of the circle being about 3 m high.

193. NETHER LARGIE, Mid Argyll
    Chambered Cairn and Cairns, sh 55, all indicated
This group of cairns, apparently set out in an almost straight
line, forms one of the most important complexes of prehistoric
monuments in Scotland. The chambered cairn of Nether Largie South is the earliest and was clearly used to receive burials
over a long period of time. Subsequent cairns were built both
to the N (at Nether Largie Mid, North and Kilmartin Glebe)
and to the S, the best preserved of which is that known as Ri
Cruin.

Nether Largie, South Cairn (NR 828979) offers one of the
best impressions of the internal arrangements of a chambered
tomb of the *Clyde* type; set within a grass-covered cairn the
chamber, partly restored, is still roofed and is divided into four
burial compartments. Excavation in 1864 revealed traces of
burials, with neolithic and beaker pottery. Two later cists were
inserted into the cairn and its present round shape may be due
to modifications at this stage. That to the N of the chamber (no
longer visible) contained a food vessel; the other, on the SW, is
still intact, but its contents had been disturbed before the
excavation.

Situated 400 m to the NNE, Nether Largie, Mid Cairn (NR
830983) measures about 30 m in diameter, but is the least
satisfying of the group to visit. When excavated in 1929 two
cists were discovered, and the position of the more northerly is
now indicated by four concrete pillars; this cist had grooved
side slabs to accommodate the end slabs. The other cist on the
S edge of the cairn is still visible; there is a cup-marking and a
possible axe carving on the NW end slab.

A further 180 m to NNE, Nether Largie, North Cairn (NR
830984) measures over 20 m in diameter, and about 3 m in
height; it covers an unusual cist at its centre, now accessible
through a roof hatch. The cist was covered by a large slab, on

193 (s cairn)

which are carved at least ten axes and some forty cup-markings. One of the end slabs is also decorated, in this case with two axe heads. The cist contained an unaccompanied inhumation burial.

The visitor who intends to continue to the Glebe Cairn should return to the village and follow the signposted access from close to the petrol station situated just beyond Kilmartin.

SDD: all times without charge.

194. RI CRUIN, Mid Argyll
    Cairn NR 825971, sh 55, Cairn

This cairn is about 20 m in diameter and has covered three cists. The most northerly cist, which contained a cremation, uses a carpentry technique in its construction and one end slab is inserted into pecked grooves in the side slabs. There are similar grooves at the E end of the cist on the s perimeter of the cairn. The w end-slab is decorated with the carving of seven flat axes. At the E end there was formerly a narrow upright slab decorated with what has been interpreted both as a boat and as a beribboned halberd. Just to the N of this cist and set within a line of boulders indicating the line of the original kerb of the cairn there are two side slabs of a third cist, again with vertical grooves at one end.

s DD: all times without charge.

195. STRONTOILLER, Lorn
Stone Circle, Cairn and Standing Stone NM 906291 and
NM 907289, sh 47, Stone Circle, Standing Stone

There is an attractive group of Bronze Age monuments to the s of Strontoiller farmhouse comprising one of the few stone circles in Argyll, a ring of thirty-one boulders some 20 m in diameter, a small kerb-cairn and an impressive standing stone, over 4 m in height. The pillar is known as Diarmid's Stone and the cairn has popularly been thought of as the burial place of the Irish hero.

196. TEMPLE WOOD, Mid Argyll
Stone Circles and Standing Stones NR 826978 and
827977, sh 55, Stone Circle, Standing Stones

There are two stone circles in a wood to the w side of the road between Nether Largie and Slockavullin. The earlier circle was discovered in the course of recent excavations and has been partially restored; it measured about 10.5 m by 10 m.

The second circle of stones, some 12.2 m in diameter, has formed an impressive enclosure within and around which burial and ritual activities have been undertaken over a long period of time. Several burial settings, now concealed beneath the stones of a covering cairn, were discovered, including a small cairn outside the circle on the NE which covered a cist with a beaker and several finely fashioned flint arrowheads.

The massive cist at the centre of the circle, within a separate stone setting, had already been rifled by the last century. One of the stones on the N side of the circle is decorated with a pecked spiral motif, one part of the spiral on one face and the other half on another.

This site and the nearby standing stones, to which access is not normally possible, have been interpreted as aspects of a 'lunar observatory', though it is perhaps more likely that the stones were erected for more mundane functions. The central stone is surrounded by four smaller stones with pairs of stones 36 m to the ENE and WSW respectively. Both the central stone and one of the latter group are decorated with cup-and-ring markings and with plain cups.

s DD: stone circles only, all times without charge.

197. TIREFOUR, Lismore, Lorn
    Broch NM 867429, sh 47, Tirefour Castle, Broch
This well-preserved broch occupies a magnificent position on
the E coast of the island of Lismore. The thick wall still stands
to a height of up to 5 m and encloses a central area some 12 m in
diameter. This broch belongs to a building tradition in which
the base of the wall is solid rather than hollow, and this no
doubt accounts in part for its preservation. A gallery within the
wall can, however, be seen at a rather higher level. Unfortunately the entrance passage is now in a disturbed condition.

46. *Clydesdale* (formerly Lanark)

198. ARBORY HILL
    Fort NS 944238, sh 72, Fort
On the summit of Arbory Hill there is a series of defences
representing two periods of fortification; the earlier, a bivallate fort encloses an area some 80 m by 70 m and has five
entrances; the later, a circular stone-walled fort, is set within
the earthworks and measures about 43 m internally. A further
bank across the line of easiest access provides an additional
defence on the E.

199. BLACK HILL
    Cairn and Fort NS 831435, sh 72, Fort
On the summit of Black Hill, a site more often visited because
of its panoramic viewpoint, there are the remains of a cairn
(some 18 m in diameter and about 1 m high) which stands
within a stone-walled fort, measuring 155 m by 110 m internally. On the SE side of the fort there is a later settlement
enclosed by an earthwork.
    National Trust for Scotland: all times without charge.

200. CAIRN TABLE
    Cairns NS 724242, sh 71, Cairns
There are two cairns on the summit of Cairn Table astride the
Clydesdale and Cumnock and Doon district boundary; the
better preserved is 16 m in diameter and 3.5 m high, but the
other has suffered from robbing and is now 12 m in diameter
and up to 1 m high.

201. CHESTER HILL
    Fort NS 953395, sh 72, Fort
On the summit of Chester Hill there is a bivallate circular fort
measuring about 85 m in internal diameter, the inner rampart
still stands to a height of about 2.5 m above the bottom of the
medial ditch.

202. FALLBURN
Fort NS 961367, sh 72, Fort

This well-preserved fort has an unusual low lying position and is situated close to the path to the summit of Tinto Hill; there are double ramparts and ditches with two entrances. The inner rampart is surmounted by a later defensive wall.

203. MID HILL, Crawford
Unenclosed Platform Settlement NS 942202, sh 72, not marked

The distinctive platforms, which are partly quarried into the hillside and partly built up to provide level stances for timber houses are clearly visible from the A74 on the NW side of Mid Hill. There are over a dozen platforms, the largest measuring 15 m by 11.5 m, disposed in lines running along the hillside.

204. NORMANGILL
Henge Monument NS 972221, sh 72, Henge

The bank and ditch of this henge monument have been cut through by the road from Crawford to the Camps Reservoir, but the opposing entrance causeways are still clearly visible on the NNW and SSE. The interior measures about 60 m by 55 m.

205. NORMANGILL RIG
Unenclosed Platform Settlements NS 966215 and 971211, sh 72, not marked

There are two unenclosed platform settlements on the hillside to the N of the road between Midlock farm, Crawford and Whelphill farm. The first is rather less than 1 km ENE of Midlock and a little to the E of a plantation, and comprises eight platforms; on a higher terrace to the NE, there is a group of at least fourteen cairns which are either burial places or perhaps piles of field-gathered stones. Some 250 m to the SE, there is a splendid group of platforms on which there would originally have been timber houses.

206. QUOTHQUAN LAW
Fort NS 988384, sh 72, Fort

Although the fort on Quothquan Law is not well preserved, the commanding summit is worth visiting for the views of the Clyde valley; the summit fort measures about 120 m by 70 m and there is a better preserved annexe on the NW side with the remains of seven house platforms.

37. Cunninghame

There is a guidebook to those ancient monuments of Arran in the guardianship of the Secretary of State for Scotland: *Ancient Monuments of Arran: official guide*, by Robert Mc-Lellan (1977), HMSO.

207. AUCHAGALLON, Arran
Cairn NR 892346, sh 69, Stone Circle

This cairn is impressive for its situation looking across to Kintyre and measures some 14.3 m in diameter over its kerb. Nevertheless there is a puzzling account that the cairn material may be of comparatively recent date, and the kerb-stones were once free-standing. It is perhaps most likely that this account records the addition of field-gathered stones to a ruined mound with well-preserved kerb in the last century.

SDD: all times without charge.

207

208. CARN BAN, Arran
Chambered Cairn NR 991262, sh 69, Chambered Cairn

This remote chambered cairn is situated in a Forestry Commission plantation some 1.7 km NNW of Auchareoch and, although in the guardianship of the Secretary of State for Scotland, it is primarily of interest to the student of such tombs rather than the general visitor. The cairn is 30 m in length and 18 m in breadth with a crescentic façade leading to a chamber at the NE end. The chamber had four compartments but was filled in after excavations in 1902.

SDD: all times without charge.

209. KILPATRICK, Arran
> Dun NR 906261, sh 69, Cashel,
> but the precise site is not indicated

This puzzling site lies in moorland about 0.8 km SE of Kilpatrick farm. When excavated in 1909 a large enclosure-wall taking in an area of about 0.9 ha was interpreted as a 'cashel' or a monastic settlement; today this part of the site is more often interpreted as a field-wall of comparatively recent date. The remains of the small stone-walled dun, comparable in size to many Kintyre examples, occupy a small knoll on the NW side of the enclosure; it measures about 17 m in diameter within a wall up to 4.5 m in thickness. This site too is difficult to interpret and may have been refurbished on a number of occasions; the presence of an even earlier prehistoric structure, perhaps a cairn, is suggested by the discovery of a short cist containing a cinerary urn with cremated bones, within the thickness of the wall to the W of the entrance.

SDD: all times without charge.

210. TORMORE, Arran
> Chambered Cairn NR 903310, sh 69, Burial Chamber

A well-preserved chamber belonging to a cairn of *Clyde* type is situated on an area of flat ground overlooking the Black Water; the cairn itself has largely disappeared, although it was probably at least 32 m in length, but the main burial chamber and the stones of the crescentic façade still survive. The chamber was excavated about 1901, and the objects discovered include sherds of grooved ware, a stone mace-head and two flint knives.

211. TORMORE, Arran
> Stone Circles, sh 69, Stone Circles

The circles are conventionally numbered from E to W, the opposite way from the line of approach from the main road; there is a small area for parking on the W side of the road and the circles are up to 2 km distant past the ruined cairn known as Moss Farm Road (NR 900326). Circle 5 (NR 908323), also known as 'Fingal's Cauldron Seat', is a double circle of large granite blocks; the eight stones of the inner ring have a diameter of 11.6 m, the fifteen rather smaller stones of the outer ring some 17.4 m in diameter. A ruined cist was found at the centre. The tradition that gave the name to the site concerns the giant Fingal, who is supposed to have tethered Bran, his dog, to the holed stone in the outer circle while he boiled up his cauldron on the stones of the inner circle. Circle 4 (NR 910323), a little over 100 m to the E, consists of four low granite blocks forming an ellipse with its longer axis some 6.4 m. Excavation revealed a central cist containing an inhumation, a food vessel, a bronze awl and three flint flakes.

Circle 3 (NR 910324), about 75 m to the N, is now only represented by a single upright, but there are three other stumps and traces of several other stones; two cists were discovered when the site was excavated, the central one containing an inhumation accompanied by a pot, the second, positioned off centre, contained a crouched inhumation with a few flint flakes.

Circle 2 (NR 911324) is 120 m to the ESE and measures 13.7 m in diameter; only three tall sandstone slabs remain upright but stumps of the others can still be seen. Two large stones in the circle have apparently been broken from a fallen upright and one has been perforated as if to form a mill-stone. Two cists were found, the central one containing a food vessel.

Circle 1 (NR 912323), the furthest from the main road, is in fact an ellipse measuring 14.6 m by 12.7 m, and is made up both of granite boulders and sandstone slabs.

SDD: all times without charge.

212. TORR A' CHAISTEIL, Corriecravie, Arran
      Dun NR 921232, sh 69, Dun
This dun, which occupies the top of a small hillock measured about 13.8 m in diameter within a wall up to 3.7 m in thickness; stretches of the outer face and a short run of inner facing stones remain in position. The entrance which is on the E, has been additionally protected by an outer rampart or wall.

SDD: all times without charge.

213. TORRYLIN, Arran
      Chambered Cairn NR 955211, sh 69, Chambered Cairn
This cairn, situated at the edge of a field to the s of Lagg Post Office, has been severely robbed, so much so that its original shape is uncertain. The chamber has been excavated on several occasions, latterly by Bryce in 1900, and the four compartments can still be seen.

SDD: all times without charge.

38. Dumbarton

214. GREENLAND
Cup-marked Rocks NS 434746,
sh 64, Cup & Ring marked Rocks

There are several natural rock surfaces with areas of decoration including twenty-two cup-and-ring markings with up to nine concentric rings, single cups set out in deliberate patterns, and ovals.

215. SHEEP HILL
Fort NS 434744, sh 64, Fort

This interesting vitrified fort is situated on an isolated volcanic knob overlooking the Clyde. Excavations between 1966 and 1970 have demonstrated a sequence of defence in which the earlier period is represented by the small fort occupying the summit, and the later by the wall which encloses the lower terrace to take in an area about 80 m by 50 m. The objects recovered from the excavation, including jet bracelets and glass beads, are in the Hunterian Museum, University of Glasgow.

TAYSIDE

There is a useful gazetteer, including Pictish symbol stones, *Ancient Monuments of Tayside*, by Herbert Coutts (1970), Dundee Museum and Art Gallery.

51. Angus

216. ARDESTIE
Souterrain NO 502344, sh 54, Souterrain

This souterrain is a good example of the type of underground store associated with surface buildings and dating to about the first century AD; it lacks the roof but the corbelling of the side walls, the central drain, and the complex entrance are all clearly visible. The surface stone-work is less easy to interpret, but it is possible that it represents internal divisions within a larger timber house, rather than acting as the foundation of small wigwam-like structures.

A large boulder decorated with cup-and-ring markings was found in the wall of one of the stone settings.

SDD: all times without charge.

214>

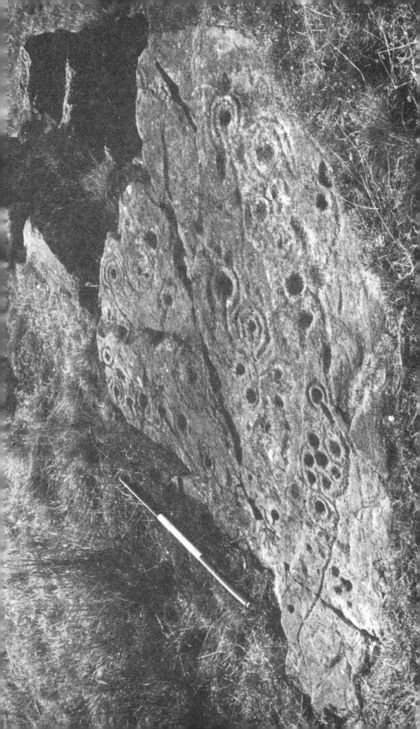

217. BARNS OF AIRLIE
        Souterrain NO 305515, sh 53, not marked
Probably the best preserved of the Angus souterrains, this site
is to be found beneath a stone dyke at the end of the second
field to the w of Barns of Airlie. The roof is virtually intact
except where a lintel has been removed to allow access; the
gallery is about 24 m long and 2 m broad. It is important to take
a torch in order to appreciate the structure fully. Excavation in
the last century revealed animal bones, querns and possibly a
bronze pin. One of the roofing slabs bears markings in the form
of serpents and cup-markings, but it is uncertain whether
these are of natural origin or are man-made.

218. BROWN and WHITE CATERTHUN
        Forts NO 555669 and 547660, sh 44,
        Brown Caterthun Fort; White Caterthun Fort
The summits of the two hills are crowned by the extensive
remains of two Iron Age hill-forts; both have a complex building sequence, but in the absence of excavation it is impossible
to suggest a firm chronological framework for their occupations. The foot paths leading to both forts can be seen on the air
photograph.

There are six lines of defence encircling the summit of the
Brown Caterthun; the innermost is a stone-walled fort, with a
gap, now considerably broadened, on the n side; this work
measures 60 m by 80 m internally. Outside it a further wall
encloses an area measuring about 185 m by 150 m; it is pierced
by no less than nine entrances, which are matched by gaps in
the twin outer ramparts with central quarry ditch. Two outer
and less regular ramparts, well-illustrated on the air photograph, occupy positions further down the flanks of the hill;
there are eight entrances through them, but, although in some
cases it is clear that the same line of access was used, they do
not match those of the inner fort.

The great mass of tumbled wall material on the White
Caterthun makes this one of the most impressive forts of
eastern Scotland to visit. The fort measures about 150 by 70 m
within a stone wall that may originally have been as much as
12 m in thickness, and it is likely that a considerable height
was achieved by the use of timber lacing. At the w end of the
interior the hollow of a rock-cut cistern, as at Finavon, may be
detected. The remains of outer ramparts and ditches, of a less
immediately defensive nature, are visible on the lower slopes.
        SDD: all times without charge.

218>

219. CARLUNGIE
  Souterrain NO 511359, sh 54, Souterrain

This complex souterrain, which is now roofless, is situated in the middle of a field to the NW of the farm, but access is possible by a narrow path through the crops. The main gallery is L-shaped with an entrance with door jambs at the E end, but there is also another narrow entrance passage and further annexes. Excavation revealed at least eight surface structures, and a cup-and-ring marked stone was found in the gallery. As at Ardestie, this souterrain was partially dismantled and filled in deliberately in antiquity. The souterrain may have served as the store-rooms and working areas for timber houses at ground level, but these have not survived.

  SDD: all times without charge.

220. FINAVON
  Fort NO 506556, sh 54, Fort

This fort, which is most readily approached from the N side by way of a gate at NO 503557, is oblong on plan measuring 153 m by 36 m within a massive timber-laced wall up to 6 m in thickness. Large amounts of vitrified material can still be seen amid the turf-covered remains.

  Excavation within the interior revealed two wells, one at the E end, the other at the W, and hearths, but it is likely that more extensive excavation would add considerably to our knowledge of the internal arrangements of the fort.

221. MAIDEN CASTLE, Carlingheugh Bay
  Fort NO 668420, sh 54, not marked

This promontory fort, which is situated at the S end of Carlingheugh Bay and E of the cliff path from Arbroath, is defended by an impressive rampart with an outer ditch. Such sites, particularly on the E and N coasts of Scotland, enclose much smaller areas than they did originally because of the depradations of coastal erosion.

222. TURIN HILL
  Fort NO 514535, sh 54, Kemp's Castle, Forts

The fortifications on Turin Hill are difficult to interpret, but the site is worth visiting for the view alone. A large oval enclosure with double ramparts was succeeded by a smaller stone-walled fort measuring about 150 m by 40 m internally. Subsequently a dun-like structure was built on the summit of the hill, partly overlying the wall of the second fort; it measures about 27 m in diameter within a stone wall some 3.5 m in thickness and the entrance is on the SW.

52. City of Dundee

223. LAWS HILL, Monifieth
Fort and Broch NO 491349, sh 54, Fort & Broch

This fort occupies the whole of the summit of Laws Hill; it measures 120 m by 60 m within a stout timber-laced wall some 9 m in thickness and there are additional defences at each end. When the fort was excavated large lumps of vitrified material were discovered, but the inner face of the wall is still comparatively well preserved in places. The lowest courses of a broch, built within the interior of the earlier fort may still be seen; it measured about 10.5 m within a wall some 5 m in thickness.

224. TEALING
Souterrain NO 412381, sh 54, Souterrain

This unroofed souterrain, situated in a field to the w of the farm, measures 24 m in length. The entrance passage into the souterrain is well preserved, with a large boulder decorated with cup-and-ring markings forming the lowest course on the N side.

No visitor should ignore the charming dovecot of late 16th-century date by the farm.

SDD: all times without charge.

225. WEST MAINS, Auchterhouse
Cairn NO 315376, sh 53, Cairn

This cairn, situated on the summit of the hill 700 m NNE of West Mains at a height of 289 m OD measures about 70 m in diameter by 2.5 m in height. When excavated in 1897 it was found to be of complex construction and to cover a cist containing a cremation burial accompanied by a bronze dagger with horn hilt and sheath mount.

53. Perth and Kinross

226. BALNACRAIG
Dun NN 747475, sh 52, Dun Geal

This well-preserved example of the group of duns found in Perthshire is situated on the top of a rocky knoll which is overlooked by higher ground to the N. Measuring about 20 m by 17.5 m within a stout wall up to 4.3 m in thickness, the dun is entered from the w side. There are several shieling huts of more recent date in the interior.

227. CASTLE LAW, Abernethy
Fort NO 183153, sh 58, Fort

This fort occupies a rocky summit 1.2 km sw of Abernethy, offering magnificent views over the River Tay to the N; parking, however, on the minor road between Abernethy and Strathmiglo is not easy, and the most convenient place is the wide entrance into Drumcairn. The fort measured 41 m by 15 m within a massive timber-laced wall up to 7.5 m thick. There was an additional defensive work at the w end, up to 5.5 m in thickness. Although the walls are now very tumbled, the position and the scale of the defences are impressive; the finds are now in the National Museum of Antiquities of Scotland, Edinburgh.

228. CROFT MORAIG
Stone Circle NN 797472, sh 52, not marked

Excavation in 1965 revealed a sequence of construction on this site which is of particular importance to students of stone circles. The first phase was a setting of fourteen upright timbers forming a horse-shoe 8 m by 7 m, with a hearth at its centre. In its second period there was a similar-shaped setting of eight upright stones about 7.5 m by 6 m with one of the stones in the NE quadrant decorated with cup-markings. In the third period a further ring of large stones was set up with a diameter of about 12.2 m, with a pair of outlying 'porch-like' stones in the SE quadrant. Discovered in front of each of these stones was a deep grave-pit.

229. DUNSINANE
Fort NO 213316, sh 53, Fort

This interesting fort occupies the summit of Dunsinane Hill and is worth visiting both because of the visible remains and because of the prospect from it. The fort measures 55 m by 30 m within a massive wall, which was probably timber-laced, and there are also three outer lines of defence. When the site was excavated in the last century what is described as a souterrain was revealed, but there are now no traces of it.

230. FORTINGALL
Stone Circles NN 745469, sh 52, Standing Stones

Excavations in 1970 showed that these two stone settings were subrectangular comprising eight stones with the largest uprights at the corners. The only finds were flecks of charcoal and some cremated bone. The sites appear to have been disturbed and partly buried in the last century. The third site comprises three stones in line, but it is not clear whether this is part of a further setting intended to be an alignment.

231. FOWLIS WESTER
Cairn, Stone Circle NN 924249,
sh 52, Stone Circle & Standing Stones

This little group of Bronze Age monuments, situated in moorland to the NNW of Fowlis Wester, comprises a kerb-cairn, a ruined stone circle and two standing stones in a line running approximately E and W. The kerb-cairn measures about 6 m in diameter and covered cremation burials; one of the kerbstones on the SSW side of the cairn was decorated with three cup-markings, but they are no longer visible. The cairn was originally surrounded by a circle of low stones, and some 9.5 m to the NNE there is an outlying stone about 1.8 m high.

To the W of the cairn there is a fallen stone and a ruined stone circle, with a diameter of 7.3 m. Excavation has revealed the original plan of the stone-holes and shown the presence of charcoal and cremated bone in the centre.

232. LEYS OF MARLEE
Stone Circle NO 159438, sh 53, Stone Circle

This attractive circle of six stones is now cut by the public road with three stones on each side; the two stones closest to the N side of the road have been displaced, but the proportions of the stones and the size of the circle itself are characteristic of this part of Scotland.

233. LITTLE TROCHRIE
Barrow NN 985403, sh 52, not marked

This tree-covered mound, some 35 m in diameter and 5.5 m in height, may be a further example of the large prehistoric barrows of Perthshire comparable to Pitnacree and Strathallan (the latter now destroyed), but it may also be partly natural in origin.

234. LUNDIN
Stone Circle NN 880505, sh 52, Stone Circle

This site is of interest not only as a well-preserved example of a 'four-poster' stone circle, but also because excavation has shown a sequence of ritual activities and burials associated with beaker and cinerary urn styles of pottery. Standing on a natural mound which serves to increase their sense of importance, the four stones form a setting about 4 m by 3.5 m, the tallest stone measuring over 2 m in height.

To the SE of the stone circle there is an isolated boulder bearing about 43 cup-markings.

235. MEIKLE FINDOWIE, Airlich
   Stone Circle NN 959386, sh 52, Standing Stones
This circle has an outer and an inner ring of stones; of the outer
ring, measuring 8 m in diameter, six stones remain upright, the
largest standing to a height of 1 m. The inner ring measures 3.8
m in diameter and consists of much smaller stones; it may
perhaps represent the kerb of a low central cairn.

236. MONCREIFFE HILL
   Fort NO 136199, sh 58, Fort
The fortifications on the hill-top, which is approached along a
forestry track from Craigend, are of two periods. In the earlier,
a pair of walls enclose an area measuring 170 m by 100 m.
Subsequently a stone-walled fort measuring about 50 m by
36 m within a wall 3.5 m thick was constructed. In the absence
of excavation, the dates of these two periods of building are not
known.

237. PITCUR
   Souterrain NO 252373, sh 53, Souterrain
This spectacular souterrain was discovered in 1878; it measures 58 m long, with an annexe passage at the w end some 18
m in length, and at least 15 m is still roofed with large slabs.
The souterrain has not been taken into State guardianship and
is in a sorry state of repair.

238. PITNACREE
   Barrow NN 928533, sh 52, not marked
This imposing mound of turf, which supports several large
conifers, measures about 27 m by 23 m and 2 m in height and
has on its summit a small standing stone. Excavations in 1964
revealed a complex sequence of structures including a rectangular stone mortuary enclosure within a horse-shoe shaped
bank. Two holes for what were clearly very substantial timber
uprights indicated the earliest structure on the site. Radiocarbon dates show that the various phases span the period
between about 3500 and 3000 BC.

239. QUEEN'S VIEW
   Dun NN 863601, sh 43, not marked
This well-preserved example of the duns or ring-forts of Perthshire has been included in a Forestry Commission trail; it
measures about 17 m in diameter within a wall 3 m thick.

240. ST MADOES
   Standing Stones NO 197209, sh 58, not marked
Formerly there were three stones in a line, but now only two
are standing; a particular interest of this site lies in the fact

that one of the stones bears many cup-markings.

There is a fine Pictish symbol stone near the door of the church (NO 196211).

241. SANDY ROAD, Scone
    Stone Circle NO 132264, sh 58, not marked

This little circle of boulders has been preserved within a housing scheme; seven stones with an overall diameter of about 5.5 m surrounded a cinerary urn containing a deposit of cremated bones.

WESTERN ISLES

242. BARPA LANGASS, North Uist
    Chambered Cairn NF 838657, sh 18, Chambered Cairn

The massive cairn of Barpa Langass, 25 m in diameter by over 4 m in height, contains a lintelled passage-grave. The forecourt on the E side of the cairn is still blocked and the outer part of the passage is not visible, but the inner part and the chamber are virtually intact. The chamber measures 4 m by 1.8 m and comprises seven upright slabs with dry-stone walling between them. Three massive lintels are still in position. Cremated bone, beaker pottery and flint objects were found in the chamber.

243. CALLANISH, Lewis
    Stone Circle and Chambered Cairn NB 213330,
    sh 8, Standing Stones

One of the most evocative of all prehistoric sites in Scotland, Callanish occupies a unique position in archaeological literature as the northern Stonehenge; a ring of thirteen tall standing stones around a dominating central monolith 4.75 m high, has a northern avenue and axial alignments to the east, west and south. Within the ring, and situated between its E edge and the central stone, there is a small passage-grave, which was first examined in 1857, when peat to a depth of about 1.5 m was removed from the site in order to provide fuel. The ring is rather flattened on the E side, and measures 13 m by 11 m in diameter, the tallest stone standing to a height of about 3.5 m. To the N the avenue is 8 m in width and runs for a distance of over 80 m; the alignments on the other three sides, though still built of large slabs are of shorter extent, the s alignment being some 27 m long.

The chambered tomb, set within a cairn some 7 m in diameter, uses one of the stones of the circle as its N portal stone;
the passage leads to a two compartment chamber, which is
now rather dilapidated. There is little doubt that the tomb is a
later addition to the circle. The excavation of the tomb in 1857
revealed only fragments of cremated human bone.
s D D : all time without charge (guide leaflet available).

244. CLACH AN TEAMPUILL, Taransay
        Standing Stone N B 012007, sh 18, Clach an Teampuill
Situated at the N E end of Loch na h-Uidhe, this stone may
possibly be prehistoric in origin, but it is now decorated with a
cross.

245. CLACH AN TRUSHAL, Ballantrushal, Lewis
        Standing Stone N B 375537, sh 8, Clach an Trushal
One of the tallest and most impressive standing stones in
Scotland, the Clach an Trushal measures about 6 m in height
and 1.8 m in breadth at the base.

246. CLACH AN TURSA, Carloway, Lewis
        Standing Stones N B 204429, sh 8, Clach an Tursa
Only one stone remains upright of what was a group of three,
but it is a substantial stone measuring 2.3 m in height; the two
fallen slabs are as much as 4.8 m in length.

247. CLACH MHIC LEOID, Harris
        Standing Stone N G 040972, sh 18, Clach Mhic Leoid
This impressive stone, standing to a height of 3.2 m, is situated
on the w side of Aird Nisabost.

248. CNOC FILLIBHIR, Lewis
        Stone Circle N B 225326, sh 8, Stone Circle
This double ring of stones, eight on the outer ellipse and three
on the inner, is situated on a low ridge and is one of the
best-preserved of the subsidiary circles round Callanish. The
outer ring is about 17.5 by 14 m and the inner about 9.5 m by
6.5 m, the proud stones offering an interesting variety of
shapes.

249. DUN CARLOWAY, Lewis
        Broch N B 189412, sh 8, Broch
This broch stands on a rocky knoll at a height of about 50 m O D
and is worthy of a visit not only because of the well-preserved
remains but also because of the vantage point its height offers.
The broch measures about 7.6 m in diameter within a wall up
to 3.6 m in thickness. The doorway which is substantially
intact is in the N W side, and there is a guard-cell which is
entered through the s wall of the entrance-passage. There are

three other chambers within the thickness of the wall and access to the interior of the wall at a higher level was made possible by the provision of steps from the cell on the SE side. The wall of the broch still stands to a height of over 9 m and illustrates clearly the technique of building the outer and inner wall faces with a median gallery.

SDD: all times without charge.

250. DUN TORCUILL, North Uist
      Broch NF 888737, sh 18, Dun

This broch, situated on an island on the W side of Loch an Duin, measures about 11.5 m internally within a wall up to 3.6 m in thickness. The entrance is on the NW and there is a mural cell on the SW side. The broch is a good example of the island situation of many Iron Age fortifications of the Western Isles – forts, duns and crannogs alike – often provided with a causeway linking the site to the adjacent shore.

251. GARYNAHINE, Lewis
      Stone Circle NN 229304, sh 8, Stone Circle

Although the uprights are not particularly massive, this compact oval setting (about 13 m by 9 m) is within sight of Callanish and is now within an untidy and often damp cutting in the peat; the five surviving stones surround a low central stone with what may be a small cairn round about it.

252. LOCH ROAG, Lewis
      Stone Circle NB 222326, sh 8, Stone Circle

This ring of stones, known as Cnoc Ceann a' Gharaidh, is in fact an ellipse measuring 21.5 m by 18 m; there are now five large upright stones and at least two fallen stones. When peat was cleared from the site in 1858 further stones and a central cairn were recorded.

253. MARROGH, North Uist
      Chambered Cairn NF 833696, sh 18, Chambered Cairn

This cairn, which measures about 24 m in diameter and over 4 m in height, is situated in moorland. The entrance to the chamber was between a pair of portal stones at the centre of the funnel-shaped forecourt, which was on the E side, but the passage is now partly filled with tumbled stones; its roof-lintels, however, are still in position, but those of the chamber have been displaced. The chamber is circular measuring about 3 m in diameter and is composed of massive uprights with intervening stones. The size of the two capstones that have covered the chamber is remarkable; the S stone which still rests on the original corbelling of the chamber measures some

3 m by 1.5 m and over 0.3 m in thickness.

There is an outlying standing stone 100 m sw of the cairn.

254. STEINACLEIT, Lewis

'Stone Circle' NB 396540, sh 8, Steinacleit

This site is difficult to interpret and, although it has been variously described as a stone circle, a chambered cairn and a ruined building, it appears to be the remains of a ruinous cairn measuring about 16 m in diameter with eleven kerb-stones still in position.

SDD: all times without charge.

255. UNIVAL, North Uist

Chambered Cairn NF 800668, sh 18, Chambered Cairn

This interesting cairn, situated in moorland on the sw flank of Uneval, contains both a passage-grave and an intrusive Iron Age house; the cairn is square in plan, measuring about 16 m along each side, with several retaining kerb-stones still in position, particularly on the se side. The passage-grave is situated at the centre of this side with a short passage leading to an oval chamber measuring about 1.8 m by 2.2 m.

On the NE flank of the cairn excavation revealed a cellular house of Iron Age date, and during its occupation the passage-grave appears to have been used as a cooking hollow.

About 7 m to the sw of the cairn there is a large outlying stone, which stands to a height of some 3 m.

The finds from the excavations of 1935 and 1939 are now in the National Museum of Antiquities of Scotland, Edinburgh.

254

ACKNOWLEDGEMENTS

The Publishers are particularly indebted to the Scottish Development Department (Ancient Monuments Branch) for permission to use the Crown Copyright photographs that appear on the following pages: 32, 42, 68 (foot), 70, 87, 99, 101, 104 (both), 107, 119, 127, 131, 133 (both), 145, 146, 147, 148, 151, 153, 159, 162, 166, 168, 177, 191, 193. Grateful acknowledgement is made, also, to the following bodies and individuals for permission to reproduce photographs as detailed: National Museum of Antiquities, Scotland (50 (top), 60, 62, 77 (both), 91, 129); Aberdeen Archaeological Surveys, Crown Copyright (120, 121); Society of Antiquaries of London (45 (foot), 84 (foot)); Society of Antiquaries of Scotland (69 (top); University of Dundee (2, 6); I.F.Larner (112, 173); Roger Mercer (52 (foot)); Malcolm Murray (84 (top)); Stuart Piggott (30); Graham Ritchie (24); Mick Sharp (frontispiece); the late Edwin Smith (9, 156); the *Stornoway Gazette* (29).

Grateful acknowledgement for permission to reproduce line illustrations is made to the following: Society of Antiquaries of London (40); Society of Antiquaries of Scotland (71); Central Excavation Unit (53); Miss Audrey Henshall (39, 126, 130); Ian Scott (94); Leicester University Press (72).

The help and advice of the following is recorded, with thanks: Michael Brooks, Jean Comrie, Trevor Cowie, Elizabeth Glass, Stratford Halliday, Rosemary Nickolls, Ian Ralston, Colin Renfrew, Anna Ritchie, Ian Shepherd.

INDEX OF SITES